I WROTE A BOOK.
Now What?

Beth Carter

To every aspiring, budding new writer.
Never quit. You can do this, future author!

ACKNOWLEDGMENTS

To my supportive, loving husband who is my biggest cheerleader and never complains (okay, rarely complains) about my messy notes all over the kitchen table and eating out a little too often when I'm on a deadline, which is often.

Thanks to Jo Van Arkel, Drury University professor and author. Jo had an easy, relaxed style while she taught Expository Writing and Creative Writing I & II. As a single mom who worked full time at the college, my only option was to take evening classes. Jo was always bright, cheery, and full of creativity even at eight o'clock at night. I took every class she taught, and was excited when she wrote in the margin of one of my essays that she thought a major magazine would publish it. I still have that paper with her motivational remarks. Thanks, Jo.

I owe a debt of gratitude to the late Allan Young, Ozarks Technical Community College instructor. When I decided to write my first novel, I didn't know where to begin, how to get published, whether I needed an agent, about query letters, a synopsis, and much more. One day, I received a mailing listing a six-week course at our local community college entitled "How to Write Your First Novel." I couldn't believe it. The timing was perfect. The next day, I registered for the course. Allan, who was likely eighty, was an entertaining instructor and a prolific author. He had written nearly one hundred novels and enthusiastically shared his journey. He gave me a great head start into the do's and don'ts of the publishing world. Rest in peace, Allan.

Thank you to WordEthic for editing this book on short notice, reading and rereading it, and putting that red pen to great use. Your expertise was appreciated. And...somehow I added 5,000 words *after* the manuscript was edited. If there's an error, blame me, not the editor.

A big thank you to Jaycee Delorenzo of Sweet 'n Spicy Designs for always creating stunning, beautiful book covers and for having a great deal of patience while I vacillated between color combinations. You're a pleasure to work with.

Contents

I Wrote A Book. Now What?

"If your dreams don't scare you, they are too small."
~Richard Branson

INTRODUCTION

Have you written your first manuscript but aren't sure about the next step? First, celebrate your accomplishment! Enjoy a glass of wine, get a massage, go to your favorite store, or binge watch that Netflix series you've been dying to see. Not many people finish a novel, book, or collection of short stories. It takes perseverance. It takes dedication. It takes sacrifice and a lot of solitary confinement. Before you delve into the competitive publishing world, you owe it to yourself to revel in this massive achievement. You did it. Take a bow.

After you've come down from the ceiling, allow me to embellish the famous cliché phrase, *Once upon a time... Help!* to make a point. The writing industry can be overwhelming. It's hard to know where to begin. I remember how lost I was a decade ago when I penned my debut.

As you read *I Wrote A Book. Now What?,* imagine you and I had lunch yesterday and you're replaying our conversation. After we devoured the spinach dip and agreed to refills, you asked me to tell you about my writing journey. Mid-sip, you begged me to share insider tips so you could polish your manuscript into its best, most marketable form. You wondered how to find readers, build an online platform, and whether to seek an agent, query an editor, or indie publish. I discussed my eventful path to becoming a traditionally published, now hybrid, author while we polished off every crumb.

In a nutshell, that's the impetus for this book. Chockful of writing advice, *I Wrote A Book. Now What?* will help you stay inspired, perfect your manuscript, pitch your work, and get published. Plus, writing nonfiction feeds into my proclivity for bullet points. As a novelist who is a pantser (more about that later) you would never know I enjoy this type of organization. I suppose it takes me back to my former corporate life.

With a gazillion authors on the planet, who am I to pen what I hope will be an invaluable guide for beginning writers? I know many authors who could write such a book, but they haven't, so I decided to take the plunge and jump chin-deep into the literary lake. I'm a traditionally published, multi-award-winning author of fourteen books: eight novels, one novella, four children's picture books, a gold-medal-winning cookbook, plus numerous short stories, and six-word memoirs.

Writers who've reached out have the same dream—to become published. But most don't know where to begin. If that's how you feel, this book is for you. Before I was an author, I worked in banking, healthcare marketing, and green heat for nearly two decades, which has been helpful in marketing my work. I discovered many craft books on writing seemed to focus wholly on marketing, advanced marketing at that. If you're just starting out, you aren't ready for algebra or calculus before you learn to multiply and divide. This book eases you into every aspect of a writing career.

I Wrote a Book. Now What? provides a focused action plan for getting noticed, setting up a platform, establishing an online presence, finding like-minded authors and readers, reaching out to industry professionals, and more. I enjoyed sharing my writing experience including humorous pitches to agents and editors.

Writing is a solitary journey. Be patient. This is a highly competitive industry. You do not want to get rejected over poor grammar or improper punctuation—or because you don't have an online platform. It happens, sadly. Likewise, these issues could lead to horrible reviews and derail your writing career before it begins.

So, roll up your sleeves and relish the thrilling trek. It isn't all uphill. I promise. Whether you're still crafting your first draft or have completed your amazing manuscript, read my book from cover to cover or skip to the section you need most. For instance, you may want to know how to write a query letter or what you should include on your author website—or you may be stuck and need some inspiring, motivational exercises.

I'm confident you'll soon be ready to launch yourself into the exciting world of publishing. Since I hope you're chomping at the keyboard to get started, let's begin.

A WRITER'S MISSION STATEMENT

You know how companies have mission statements that are generally dry, boring, and no one reads them? Yeah, I know, but writers have a cool one. I'm not sure who came up with the writer's mission statement below. I'd love to credit them because I think it's brilliant. Here's our mission statement:

DRINK COFFEE AND MAKE STUFF UP.

Isn't that the best? I saw this online a decade ago and couldn't love it more. I think we should all print this out and hang it in our offices.

> **"Don't be 'a writer.' Be writing."**
> **~William Faulkner**

MY POTHOLED, CURVY WRITING JOURNEY

As a single mom for sixteen years, I worked in education, banking, and healthcare marketing. In that role, I wrote many nonfiction articles, essays, interviews, profiles, newsletters, and press releases. I didn't dream of writing for fun until I approached midlife. Okay, later than midlife, but people do live to be 100, you know.

I began my fictional writing journey in 2010. I had a bumpy start right from the get-go. My first manuscript was set on a college campus—I worked on one for seven years—and I was excited to share some firsthand knowledge of professors, students, board members, and administrators. The genre was going to be romantic suspense. However, when I was more than half finished, my computer croaked, dead as an annoying gnat in my wineglass. We called the Geek Squad but they were baffled. Another tech guru couldn't fix it, so my husband sent it off to some clean computer company with a room akin to a sterilized operating room. They took my computer completely apart. I waited. And I waited. For months.

In the meantime, our family was shattered by a brutal tragedy. It was a horrific, unbelievable, shocking time. Each of us was broken and numb. I could barely function, much less write humorous scenes. We held hands at the dinner table and half expected a crime show to call. It was a devastating time. Never mind that my manuscript was lost on the stupid computer; it was an impossible time to function, let alone write. Months later, at Barnes & Noble, I spotted the children's section and smiled, remembering how much fun it was to read rhyming picture books to my toddler daughter. I crouched at a tiny kids' table and read several children's books, one after the other. People probably wondered why I was in the children's section but the kidlit brought me hope, joy, and inspiration. Children's books became my therapy after my niece's tragic death.

I chucked my novel idea, researched the word count for children's picture books, began Googling publishers, and away I went. I didn't have any idea how that world worked and soon found that an illustrator is as important as the author's words.

To date, I've written four children's books: *What Do You Want to Be?, The Missing Key, Santa's Secret*, and *Sour Power*. They are a welcome break from a long novel or a nonfiction book, and the joy I receive from reading my books to kids in elementary school is almost overwhelming. My dear, departed, beautiful niece gave me this gift. She was an avid reader, and I'd give anything if we could discuss reading and writing now. I have a feeling she'd pen her own novel. Maybe she is in heaven.

Eventually, my computer came back, amazingly fixed. My sweet husband printed my manuscript, three-hole punched it, complete with tabs, and placed it in a notebook, where it remains untouched today. I will get back to it. But after my first children's book was published, I started a new novel called *Thursdays At Coconuts*. That book now has more than 600 reviews and 1,000 ratings, and led to a six-book series including *Chaos At Coconuts* (Book 2), *Babies At Coconuts* (Book 3), *Cowboys At Coconuts*, (Book 4), and *Brides At Coconuts* (Book 5.) As of this writing, I haven't revealed the title to the final book in this series, but it'll be available this year.

I've written standalone novels, *Sleeping With Elvis* (the

hero is an Elvis impersonator), a sweet, heartwarming Christmas novella, *Miracle On Aisle Two*, and during the 2020 pandemic I penned a cookbook, *The Quarantine Cookbook*. I'm also a huge fan of six-word memoirs—more about those later—and have written several short stories and a novelette, *Santa Baby*.

I've been busy. But that's enough about me. Let's get to this thing called writing, marketing, and publishing.

WRITING ADVICE

> "Writing is the Painting of the Voice."
> ~Voltaire

FIND YOUR VOICE

Every writer has a unique voice. Some are funny, others are dark. Several are academic or technical, and many are literary. Whether you write mainstream fiction, literary fiction, a how-to book on building cars, a children's book, or a collection of poetry or short stories, there's no right or wrong. There's your voice. Period. It's important to find your own style and stick with it because readers who love your work will expect a similar voice in each book. Even though this book is nonfiction, I still infused humor and a conversational tone, just like in my novels.

I think you'll enjoy this story because it's how I imagine every writer feels after penning their first manuscript. When I wrote my debut, *Thursdays At Coconuts*, I Googled freelance editors and was lucky enough to find one who was a former women's fiction editor from St. Martin's Press. My novel was women's fiction, so I knew it would be a great fit. I hired Ms. Brown immediately to do an overall evaluation of my manuscript.

I sat on pins and needles awaiting her response and nearly made myself sick with worry. I fretted that she would hate it but secretly hoped she'd love it and connect me with an agent friend of hers, spurring me to a bestseller list right away. A girl can dream, right?

I heard back within a couple of months. She gave me thrilling feedback, saying I was a strong writer, hoped my manuscript didn't get lost in a slush pile, and suggested I make the cop more likeable, which I took to heart. The editor also suggested I begin with my fourth chapter—meaning delete the first three chapters—but, oh, my God, I loved those chapters. It was a wedding, after all, and crucial plot points occurred right away. How could I leave those out? I left them in and decided if another editor told me to delete them I would. Luckily, the editor who eventually offered a contract on my manuscript loved the first three chapters. Whew.

The women's fiction editor I hired before I landed a book deal said I needed to decide whether my voice was going to be light and humorous or dark. She said I straddled the line between suspense and humor and thought I should choose one or the other. Oh, no. I loved both styles.

At first I was annoyed—because all writers think their book baby is perfect—but as I reread her detailed comments, it occurred to me that I did include a great deal of suspense. I always have a few suspenseful scenes but have far more humorous and heartwarming ones. As I stared at her notes, a lightbulb clicked. I stared at a pile of books I hadn't yet read and realized there were far more thrillers than romance on my coffee table. I knew that was likely how my darker voice infiltrated my humorous writing. Of course, I read romance and women's fiction since that's what I mainly write. I also enjoy memoirs, biographies, and many other genres. I'll never stop reading thrillers, and maybe I'll even pen one someday, but it was the editor's insightful observation that gave me pause and made me consider my voice. Consider your voice and do your best to remain consistent.

LEARN THE LITERARY LINGO

You'll be way ahead of me if you learn writerly terms early on. I remember sitting in on writing meetings and wondering what some of the terms meant, but I didn't want to appear obtuse and didn't ask. Silly me. I should have. Instead, it took me longer to figure out by reasoning—or muddling—my way through the writing lingo.

You will hear many acronyms, abbreviations, and initialisms bandied about at local, regional, and national conferences. Don't be embarrassed to ask what they mean. Google, attend workshops, and read craft books to be seen as a knowledgeable professional. Following is not an all-inclusive list but covers many common phrases used in writing. By the way, with social media, we're all familiar with many initialisms such as LOL (laugh out loud), or ROFL, (rolling on the floor laughing).

Here are writing-related terms you'll want to know:

WIP – Work in progress. Whether you're writing a novel, a nonfiction book, cookbook, or a short story, a WIP is your work in progress.

MS – Manuscript for one book or novel.

MSS – The plural term for multiple manuscripts.

MC – Main character.

POV – Point of view. Always make it clear which character is speaking. In my *Coconuts* series, I have four main characters and weave their storylines throughout my novels. The easiest way for me to determine whose POV I'm in—and to stay in that voice—is to begin the chapter with the character who is the main focus of said chapter. That'll make it obvious to your readers as well.

Head Hopping – This is when it's not clear who is

talking. You want to ensure that you stay in your character's head and don't express another character's thoughts by accident. In my first novel, I got into trouble head hopping because my three main characters meet weekly for Happy Hour at a bar called Coconuts. As they talked, it was sometimes hard to differentiate who was speaking. This goes back to POV. Using dialogue is the easiest way to keep them separate. Also, when I have several characters in the same scene, I start off with whomever's thoughts I plan to stay in for that chapter, and other characters chime in through dialogue, not internal thoughts.

Dialogue Tags – Example: "I hope this book is helpful," Beth said. Also, "Are you learning valuable advice?" Beth asked.

"Said" and "asked" are dialogue tags. When your characters have a long conversation, if it's clear who is whom, dialogue tags can be dropped because they get monotonous for the reader and the writer.

Show Don't Tell – I think this is one of the hardest lessons for beginning writers to learn. We like to tell stories. We're storytellers. But readers want us to *show* them the story. Examples:

Telling: The new guy at work is hot.

Showing: When the new guy at work rolls up his sleeves exposing toned, tanned arms, I can't concentrate.

Which one makes you visualize him and want to know more?

HEA – Happily Ever After. This is how the majority of romance novels end, though not all. It's usually expected but not required. Just remember, readers may throw the book across the room if your hero and heroine don't get together at the end.

HFN – Happy For Now. This is now an acceptable ending, even in Romancelandia because, let's face it, a happy for now ending is more realistic.

Insta Love – Speaking of being realistic—or not—some authors write novels where a couple falls in love instantly.

Often, readers get angered by this because it doesn't seem plausible. However, I bet we all have at least one friend or relative who got hitched after a few short weeks and lived happily ever after. I know I do. Still, use this trope sparingly.

DNF – Did not finish. This is something you hope you'll never read in a review. You always want readers to finish your book. Make sure you have a riveting read that keep the pages turning.

Pantser – My readers laughed and laughed when I told them I was a pantser. I'm not sure how they pictured me— possibly without pants—because they think this term is hilarious. Every book club I've spoken to thinks it's a funny term, too, and they always ask if it's real. Yes, it is. Let me explain.

A pantser is someone who literally writes by the seat of their pants. They may start with a blank journal, legal pad, or open up the laptop and start typing after first staring at a blank page. It's exhilarating. And terrifying. I'm a pantser through and through and get myself into a lot of trouble for it. I write repeat scenes, I get my timeline out of order, and when I'm finished with an 85,000-word novel, I generally have to put it together like an intricate jigsaw puzzle with tiny pieces.

You might wonder why I'd put myself through all that. It's because I'm truly surprised by my characters. I may think they're going to turn right and they decide to go left into unchartered territory. New characters pop up, flat tires happen, or a past enemy is hitchhiking. None of this has happened, well, actually, all of it has except for the hitchhiker, which gives me a story idea, but I digress. When I write like a reader reads, it means I'm going to be surprised as well. I've had characters veer way off course, come back to life after I killed them, and I don't write soap operas. It's that much fun, that difficult, but oh, so rewarding.

Plotter – A plotter has fun too, I'm sure, but when I see an author's colorful Post-it notes, one for character names, one for plot, one for the villain, and so on, it makes my head hurt. Some authors make spreadsheets to keep their chapters straight and already know what will be in each chapter before they're written. What? I don't even number my chapters until I write "The End." Because, as I mentioned previously, my work is always out of order.

I have several author friends who are plotters and just as many who are pantsers. Plotters want pantsers to try their way and vice versa. Plotters, I see your fancy Excel spreadsheets and color-coded chapters and raise my Ziploc baggies full of plot points on napkins, receipts, and Post-its. I've even been known to pull into a parking lot and write an idea on my palm. I'm old school, but it works for me.

You simply have to find the system that works best for you. Don't fight it if you're the spreadsheet type who loves bullet points and presentations. I won't tell.

Plantser – Aha! A plantser is a happy medium, a combination of plotter and pantser. I have to admit, much to my chagrin, that with my *Coconuts* series, I've had to force myself to make bullet points to keep a few stray, secondary plot threads straight so I wouldn't forget to address them in the next book. Who knows, maybe I'll find this method to be the most effective way to write. Doubtful, though. I love the surprise of being a pantser.

ARC – Advanced Reader Copy – This is what you send to trusted readers to get feedback on your manuscript and early reviews. If you decide to entrust your manuscript to early readers before you send it to an agent or editor, it's up to you whether you send two, ten, or twenty-five ARCs. Just remember that you'll receive a variety of comments from each person, and if you've written a 400-page novel, it will take an enormous amount of time to wade through all the responses. I generally send three or four ARCs to trusted beta readers who are avid readers, and it helps if they're proficient with grammar and punctuation. I don't usually have an issue in those areas, but I guarantee you each beta will find something different in every novel, sometimes even after two editors have gone through it. I'm always amazed.

Beta Readers – Basically, these are mystical creatures

—kidding!—who are good with finding inconsistencies. Maybe you said the heroine has green eyes in the beginning and toward the end you describe them as sky blue. After writing three or four hundred pages with multiple characters, it's easy to make these mistakes. Beta readers will also provide valuable feedback regarding your plot and character development, what they enjoyed—or disliked, and if a certain villain drove them to drink.

Hero – This is the hero who saves the day. In *Sleeping With Elvis*, my hero is a hunky Elvis impersonator who has a cursing parrot. It doesn't get much better than that. Heroes come in many different forms—a man, woman, pet, fireman, teacher, or healthcare worker, to name a few.

Heroine – The heroine is the female lead. In historicals, this might be a damsel in distress or it might be a landowner fighting off the bad guys. In a contemporary, the heroine could be a freaking mess in her personal life but a professional CEO who runs a thriving company.

Alpha – This could be your tough-talking, kickass cop or an entrepreneur, male or female, of course.

Beta – A beta character always reminds me of the reliable, sweet boy or girl next door. Not aggressive, and possibly not even assertive, but steady as a rock. It's up to you to create the type of characters you prefer. As in real life, it's always best to have a mix.

Villain – Everyone knows what a villain is. Hopefully, you've never dated one. I have more fun creating villains, probably because I'm a sweet, rather southern woman, who often bites her tongue rather than having conflict, especially in public. Creating a nasty villain helps me vent.

Echoes – Echoes are pesky repetitive words that we often miss. We all have words we favor and use often. The trick is to not have the same, repetitive words on the same page, or worse, in the same paragraph. After writing a couple hundred pages, it's easy to glaze over these. Editors will often find them, but it's better if you do first. One easy way is to click on the "Find" button and type in a word you use often.

See how many times it pops up, and use a synonym in its place.

Purple Prose – Writers and readers love detail. It sets the scene and the tone, but don't go overboard. I read a book that spent two chapters talking about a black bra. It was totally over the top and reviewers noticed it too. Know when the description is enough. If you're using extreme amounts of flowery adjectives and adverbs, you likely have purple prose.

Kill Your Darlings – I'm not wild about this phrase but it means to edit your work ruthlessly and cut, cut, cut. We all tend to fall in love with our words and our characters, but like the black bra example, know when you've gone overboard. It's much better to tighten the prose, get the point across, and move the story forward.

Plot Points – These are the major scenes and chapters you plan to incorporate in your novel. A plot point might be about a wedding, a bank robbery, a school dance, a touching proposal, or a disastrous date. Let your imagination run wild.

Plot Holes – This is where you unknowingly leave a reader hanging—unless you intend to address these issues later with a serial novel or series of books. Make sure you don't leave major threads open or readers will be unsatisfied and unhappy.

Timelines – I've only had an issue with timelines once that I'm aware of. It was for my debut novel, *Thursdays At Coconuts*, since my characters met every Thursday for Happy Hour. I found it difficult to navigate around school days and weekends for my high school counselor. I literally had to create a timeline and count the days of the week to correct the issue. For this reason, I now avoid happenings on a certain day of the week.

Critique Groups – I am friends with authors from Arkansas who, pre-Covid, met weekly for critique sessions. They each brought five to ten typewritten pages of their WIP, passed them around, and offered helpful critique. I was slightly jealous I didn't have a group like this in Missouri, although I did attend a monthly romance writers' group in the early years that did this before every meeting. The problem was there were at least thirty writers in the room. That's lot of differing opinions, not to mention paper to print out. I think critique groups work best in a tightknit setting with five to ten writers. Online critique groups are a thing too. Search your area to see if there are already groups or start your own.

First Person – This is where your main character is telling the story by using the word "I" throughout. Examples: "I told Ben I was unfulfilled in our relationship." Or "After Ben was a jerk, I broke up with him." Note: I only know nice men named Ben. But don't get me started ...never mind.

Third Person – When writing in third person, you only use "I" when the character is expressing something via dialogue or in their internal thoughts. Otherwise, your characters are always called by their names or nicknames. With novels, I write in third person; with nonfiction, I write in first. Many authors write novels using first person. It's entirely a preference and is up to you.

Passive Writing – Passive writing is exactly what it says—passive. The easiest way to make sure you aren't writing passively is to remove the word "was." Use Find to see how many times you used "was." It's probably a lot, or at least that was an issue with my first manuscript. Here's an example of passive writing.

Passive: I was driving to the store.

Better: I drove to the store.

See the difference? It's more urgent. That's a boring example, but you get the gist. You could beef it up by adding:

I drove to the store on two wheels, late as usual, before screeching to a halt when a child ran into the road.

This sentence immediately paints an urgent, heart-pounding picture.

Present Tense – Happening in the present. I know several authors who write in present tense. I can't seem to get my English teacher off my shoulder to do this. It seems like poor grammar, but my author friends insist it creates action and urgency for the reader, i.e., "I set my coffee mug on the table and observe deer in the back yard."

Paste Tense – Happened in the past. This is my preference. Using the above example, I'd say: "I sat my coffee mug on the table and observed deer in the back yard." There's no right or wrong. Whichever tense you prefer is entirely up to you. If you thumb through well-known authors' books, you'll notice both tenses are used. Be careful not to mix them, though.

Omniscient – Isn't that an interesting word? It means the work is told from an all-knowing, sort of God-like perspective. I've heard readers and writers say they feel disconnected from the characters and the book when this style is used.

Become familiar with these terms. I'm sure there are many more which you can easily Google, but this book can only be so long. You will come off as polished and professional if you already know these terms. It took me three writers' groups and two novels before I understood them all.

LET'S DISCUSS WORD COUNT

This may sound simplistic, and you hopefully already know how long your book should be according to standard guidelines. If not, word count varies widely depending on the genre. You certainly don't want to risk being rejected simply because your novel is much too long or too short. Don't make that mistake. Your time is too valuable.

As mentioned earlier, I write humorous, romantic women's fiction, which is home to one of the longer word counts. Luckily, I overwrite by a lot and tend to be chatty—at least my characters are. For my genre, the word count is generally 80,000 to 100,000 words. Most of my novels come in around 85k.

Here's a general guide to word count per genre:

Novels: 80-100,000. Includes romance, thrillers, suspense, mystery, women's, literary, and mainstream.

Chick Lit: 70-75,000. For some reason, they're often a bit shorter.

Westerns: 50-80,000. This genre also touts shorter books.

Sci-Fi and Fantasy: 100-115,000. Higher counts are allowed due to necessary world building.

Middle Grade (MG): 20-55,000. Kids are voracious readers but may not have the staying power adults have.

Upper Middle Grade: 40-55,000. For tweens.

Young Adult (YA): 55-80,000.

Memoir: 80,000-90,000.

Children's Picture Books (PB): 500-600. Sounds easy,

right? It isn't, especially if you write in verse. Two of my children's books are written in verse and two are not. I have one PB that's 1,000 words. That pushed the limit, because with kid lit you have to allow ample room for illustrations, which are as important as the words in telling the story. Also, if children are just beginning to read, they might be overwhelmed with a long book. Likewise, tired parents who read these books to their children at bedtime over and over will thank you for fewer words.

Nonfiction Books: 20,0000-50,000. This is my best guesstimate after buying many craft books over the years. Some are as thick as novels but many are half that length, especially if the author plans to build on the subject matter in subsequent books.

Cookbooks: 100-200 pages. My cookbook, *The Quarantine Cookbook*, has nearly 200 recipes, six-word memoirs on quarantine life, many sheltering-in-place suggestions, and humorous food quotations. My cookbook is 227 pages long and was great fun to write. And, I'm told, to read.

Of course, there are always exceptions to every rule just to keep us on our toes, but longer books are more expensive for a publisher to print, plus it takes more time for everyone involved to edit. Time is money, as someone once said.

Use this guide as a reference. I prefer to overwrite the first draft—sometimes by 20,000 words—and either move big sections to a sequel or cut scenes altogether. But that's just me.

Source: *Writer's Digest* February 5, 2021, article by Chuck Sambuchino. To save space, I paraphrased and rounded off their recommendations.

KEEP TRACK OF CHARACTER NAMES

You'll want to write down the names of your characters for each book you write. After seven or eight books, it's easy to forget what you've used and have duplications. I believe I've used the name Mia twice in two different novels. Obviously, I like that name but need to retire it.

With my debut, Thursdays At Coconuts, the editor asked if I realized I had seven character names beginning with "S." No, I did not. She asked me to change a few of them, saying readers might get confused, so, of course, I did. I didn't notice how I had favored the letter "S" since only one was a main character. I kept Suzy, the wedding planner, and Sean, a cop's egotistical brother. I changed Sara to Tara (clever, right?) and swapped Sylvia with Emma. I honestly can't remember what the other "S" names were but they were switched as well.

If I had made a list of my characters' names to begin with, I would have caught this. I rarely use surnames, unless the character is called by name, i.e., Miss Truman, high school guidance counselor, Lt. Tony Montgomery, a cop; or Cole Cash, a dirt-poor cowboy. I loved both the alliteration of his name and the fact that he doesn't have money. You can have a lot of fun with ironic names that way.

CREATE A LIST OF RESTAURANTS/STORES/ SHOPS

Just like character names, after several books, it's easy to forget what you named a particular restaurant, bar, tire shop, or salon. If you're writing a series this is especially important to remember, so jot down a list in a journal or create a file on your computer.

With my *Coconuts* series, I kept adding new places for the characters to visit. I finally created a file and made a list because I began to forget the names of these establishments after five novels. Here are a few from all of my novels:

Coconuts - The best friends' main hang-out, a bar/restaurant.

Maria's Mexican Restaurant - A favorite among some of my characters.

The Coffee Drip – A cute coffee shop.

Crystal City Diner - My novel is set in Crystal City.

Lefty's – A dive bar with live music.

Key Lime Bistro – A bistro with a lime green theme to go with my novel, *Sleeping With Elvis*, which is set on Key Lime Island.

Key Lime Ice Cream Shoppe - An adorable ice cream shop on the beach in *Sleeping With Elvis*.

Bottoms Up - A bar where two of my characters meet in my holiday novella, *Miracle On Aisle Two*.

Those are but a few. I'm currently running a contest for readers to name a country hair salon and will probably ask them to name a dog for a new secondary character. Get people involved. They'll love the challenge and will become invested in your work. Besides, readers come up with awesome names.

DIFFERENTIATE YOUR CHARACTERS

Character development is extremely important. You want them all to be vastly different and distinguishable from one another. Cardboard characters will not keep readers coming back for more. They need to be able to relate to your characters—whether they love them or hate them. Writers need to drag their characters through the mud and eventually have them get back up again. When I heard a reader, Kim, say, "I half expect your characters to friend or tag me on Facebook," I knew I'd created realistic characters. Some have said they'd love to have a cocktail with my main characters. Others want to throw a drink in the face of my villains. Again, that's what you want if you're writing fiction.

When I wrote my debut, I created Character Description Forms, made several copies for each character, and dutifully filled them out. Now, I add the information in a Word document. In addition to the standard hair and eye color, height, weight, marital status, and whether they have kids or pets, also describe where your characters live, if they cook, their favorite food and drinks, any sibling rivalries, and so on. You'll forget details long this if you have a big cast of characters and a long series, believe me.

You want to get to know your characters' thoughts, emotions, fears, and quirks. Are they night owls or early birds? Introverted or extroverted? Were they popular in high school or wallflowers? Really get to know their backgrounds and what drives them. My friend and author, Jan Morrill, actually interviews her characters. I attended one of her presentations and learned she has written a book about this topic called *Creative Characterization.*

Here are several ways to differentiate your characters:

Profession – Have both professional and blue-collar employees. Moms and dads, scientists, construction workers, doctors, nannies, or engineers. Mix it up. In my *Coconuts* series, one of my characters, Suzy, is a wedding planner. Alex is a bank marketer who dates a bad-boy cop, and Hope is a high school counselor who has hippie parents. Cheri is a New York socialite with absentee parents who travel abroad. They're all vastly different as far as their careers and personalities, yet they're the best of friends.

Age – Don't have all twenty-something characters or surly teens. Add a granny or a grumpy old neighbor to enrich your writing. Seasoned romance novels with older couples are popular, especially as Baby Boomers age.

Marital Status – Some of my characters are married, and others are single or divorced. It's always better to have a variety, just like in real life.

Kids – Know-it-all teens make great secondary characters, as do fussy babies or cute toddlers.

No Children – Characters who choose not to have children and throw themselves in their careers are equally compelling. You may have a character who suffers from infertility issues or has difficulty adopting a child. Readers enjoy reading about real-life, relatable challenges.

Race – Having diverse characters with a variety of ethnic backgrounds is more realistic and enjoyable to write.

Pets – I wrote about a cursing parrot in *Sleeping With Elvis*, and she became a major secondary character. Readers loved her.

International Characters – I have a French fashion designer in my *Coconuts* series, a fiery Irish chef, and several Italian family members. They're all bilingual and speak English but often revert to their native language, especially if they're upset. I handle this by sprinkling in commonly known terms in their dialogue like *oui, bonjour,* and *ciao.* You don't want to use so many terms that readers have to stop reading the story in order to research the phrase, though. Use these words sparingly.

Type A Personality – We all know this person. I might be this person. These people are focused, often leaders, and usually perfectionists.

Type B Personality – You immediately have conflict when you pair a relaxed, happy-go-lucky Type B character with an uptight, overachieving Type A character. That's when the fun begins for an author.

Relatable – We see plenty of sexy men and women on book covers. Also use relatable characters that may have issues with their weight, a balding head, lack organizational skills, don't get along with family members, or hate their job. Give every character faults or quirks to make them endearing and interesting. You cannot have all perfect, beautiful, sexy characters. It isn't realistic.

Self-Deprecating – My character, Hope, hates her name, looks, and hair. When I ask readers which of my characters they like the most, it's almost always Hope. When characters are self-effacing and flawed, most readers will relate to them.

Drinks – Southerners drink sweet tea; a friend from the UK often drinks G&T (gin and tonic.) Study specific drinks for specific regions or countries. This is a great way to differentiate characters. I have one character who loves margaritas and my four BFFs always drink Angry Balls when they're having relationship issues. Isn't that the best name?

Hobbies – Give your characters hobbies and interests to make them appear to jump off the page.

Quirks – Bank marketer Alex has a touch of OCD and has rituals such as tying paper straw holders into knots. I also do this. We all loved Lucy who constantly bumped into things or fell down. Readers love bumbling, silly, imperfect characters.

Fears – Pepper, the heroine in *Sleeping With Elvis*, is extremely fearful of flying and boating. Yet, as a kindergarten teacher who tells kids to dream big, she forced herself to do both.

Dialect and Slang – Cole, the cowboy in my *Coconuts* series always drops his g's. Five-year-old Betsy, in *Miracle On Aisle Two*, cannot pronounce the letter r, as in Mewwy Cwismas. Using slang, can cause an editing nightmare, especially with autocorrect, but it definitely helps to differentiate characters.

Nicknames – Cowboy Cole gets into a relationship with the socialite—the always fun, lively opposites attract trope. He calls her New York; she in turn calls him Cowboy. Most of us use nicknames in relationships. They're cute, plus it breaks the monotony of using the same character name over and over.

Attire – My hippie art teacher in *Coconuts*, Willow, wears a gazillion bangle bracelets. Cheri, the New York socialite, almost always wears animal print. Hope, the high school guidance counselor, wears Capri pants, blouses, and sensible, flat shoes. This helps readers envision them and aids the writer in keeping them straight when several characters are in the same scene.

Unique Hairstyles – Some might shave their head, others might have a Mohawk, mullet, or never be without a ponytail. Characters could have pink hair, an old-fashioned bee hive up-do, or prematurely gray hair or no hair—just like in real life.

Childhood and Upbringing – A character's childhood and upbringing is often an aha moment when bits of backstory are revealed to explain the character's motive.

These are just a few examples to help you develop your characters more fully. Combine several of these options, mix and match, and you'll have character material for life.

ADD MUSIC

I've always used music to set the tone for a celebration. When my husband turned sixty, I planned a surprise party and asked everyone to dress in sixties garb. A few months beforehand, I listened to 60s music for inspiration. I made notes of the songs I wanted to use and even had CDs made, complete with tie-dye and peace sign covers. And here I thought all of the best music was during the 70s.

When I got remarried after sixteen long years, and two broken engagements (by me), I requested the vocalist sing "At Last" by Etta James when my mother and grandmother were escorted down the aisle. I thought it would be hilarious, and it was. I'll probably do that again for a character who has either never married or has gone years in between marriages.

For my writing, I also research songs. Many, many songs. If I'm writing about a cowboy, like in my novel, *Cowboys At Coconuts*, I exclusively listen to country music to get in the mood for all things country. Either that, or I'll drive to my parents' farm and sit a spell.

While writing about a concert where my Elvis impersonator in *Sleeping With Elvis* performs in Branson, you guessed it, I listened to music by The King. I learned three of Elvis's Grammy awards were for gospel songs. Isn't that interesting?

Michael Jackson's "Thriller" makes an appearance at a Halloween wedding in *Chaos At Coconuts*, as well as the spooky "Love Song for A Vampire" by Annie Lennox, which was the perfect song for the fork-tongued bride's bridal march.

Of course, I incorporated several holiday songs in *Miracle On Aisle Two* where my five-year-old character,

Betsy, belts out "Mewwy Cwismas." I also added countless steering-wheel-thumping, foot-tapping sixties and seventies songs blasted from the hippies' VW Microbus in my *Coconuts* series over the course of several books.

Whatever genre you write, try adding a few songs to energize your work—and yourself. Be sure to put titles in quotation marks and always give the artist credit. If you list an entire album, that should be in italics. My understanding is authors should not include lyrics—or even a portion of lyrics—just as we wouldn't want someone to plagiarize our words. In fact, my editor took creepy, voice mail lyrics out of my debut, *Thursdays At Coconuts*, until I told her I wrote them myself. Back in they went.

Have fun with the tunes. At the very least, listening to music will brighten your mood while on deadline.

UTILIZE WEATHER

One thing about weather, it's universal. Every single one of us can relate to various storms, floods, tornadoes, hurricanes, and snowstorms. If you're writing a novel, don't forget to include the weather. Not every day will be sunny and bright, even in your fictional world. Most of us are riveted by nonstop weather coverage. Be sure to include weather to ensure realism.

If you ever plan to include a hurricane, before one hits is the time to notice the evacuation signs and routes, the unfortunate price gouging, the mad packing and stuffing of cars/vans/RVs, the 24/7 news coverage, covered windows, as well as the un-boarded homes from the I'm-riding-this-out-no-matter-what folks. During these times, you'll also notice sand bags, never-ending lines of traffic, looming, swirling radar on the television screen, state and national action plans, as well as the wonderful people like the Red Cross, Convoy of Hope, Cajun Navy, storm chasers, reporters, meteorologists and others who drive into these scary areas to provide crucial aid.

Writing about bad weather—*really* bad weather—will guarantee tension and conflict in your work. After all, our characters can't always have blue skies while sitting on the porch sipping lemonade and petting the dog—or while sipping wine and cuddling with a loved one. Eventually, even rainbows and unicorns become monotonous. Writers simply can't forget the darker side of reality.

Beyond thunderstorms, I've used a variety of severe weather situations in my novels. Now, I wonder whether this is because I dated a meteorologist for years, but I digress. Here are some examples of weather-related scenes in my work:

Chaos At Coconuts

A tornado provided the outlet for a *major* plot twist in *Chaos At Coconuts*. Before I wrote this novel, I wondered how I would achieve this particular shock and awe moment, and my fictional twister delivered the perfect platform. It helped that I live in Missouri where we have tornadoes annually. I've helped with cleanup in my town and saw the aftermath of the EF5 tornado in Joplin, where trees were stripped of bark and houses were flattened to their foundations. Even though tornadic events are heart wrenching, they can provide many heartwarming scenes.

Sleeping With Elvis

I created a deadly tropical storm at sea that allowed me to create tension and plot twists for the characters traveling aboard a charter to Key Lime Island. I researched Coast Guard lingo, plus being married to a husband who has taken captain courses helped immensely. We boat often and it was easy for me to describe the water sloshing over the sides, darkened skies, lightning zigzagging, losing sight of land, the rocking, slippery boat, and much more.

AVOID EDITING WHILE WRITING

I know authors who edit as they write, no matter what experts recommend. They simply cannot resist rereading every sentence or paragraph and reworking it until they get it just so. But therein lies the problem.

By doing this, these authors take *forever* to finish their books, or worse, years later, they're still tweaking instead of submitting. I know someone like this who has written more than 400,000 words for one book, and he's *still* writing this tome. I asked why he didn't divide it into four or five books and mentioned he'd already have a built-in series that he could release quickly. He wasn't interested. He wants to create another *War and Peace*, I suppose. By the way, Tolstoy's word count for that book is 587,287 words. And I thought I was verbose.

I never edit as I go unless I happen to see a word underlined in red and can quickly correct the typo before moving on. I also never rework sentences or move paragraphs, scenes, or chapters until nearly the end. Many authors cannot write unless it's in a linear fashion from beginning to end. This is all a matter of style and choice. There's no right or wrong way to pen a book. Write in a way that's the most comfortable for you.

As a pantser, I fully admit, my brain doesn't work in an organized manner. I tend to write in crop circles or something akin to the Olympic rings. I occasionally describe this as wrestling a ravenous Grizzly. Never fear, I always win—even though at times, I think the bear will defeat me. When my draft is finished, I spend a month or two piecing together this self-inflicted, gigantic jigsaw puzzle called a manuscript, but it works for me. I've written multiple novels and have won several national and international awards.

If, on the other hand, you are a plotter, super organized, and write in a linear fashion, I bow to you. I admire writers who start with page one and journey through, in order, until they pen "The End." I am not that type of writer. My brain must be spastic. I simply wanted you to know there are different writing styles and it works best when you don't fight your natural process.

Finally, as Janet Evanovich said in her writing craft book, *How I Write: Secrets of a Bestselling Author,* and I'm paraphrasing here, "Vomit out the first draft." Even though the visual induces a chuckle and face scrunching, I agree with her sentiment. As I mentioned, all writers have their own system, so do whatever works best for you. However, I truly think you'll have a better outcome if you let the words soar before you tinker with them.

STRENGTHEN YOUR VERBS

When I submitted my debut novel years ago, my editor said I used these three words much too often: walked, looked, and small. After 350 pages, you don't realize your characters may be walking and looking far too much. And apparently the three best friends thought everything was small. Hey, this isn't what you are thinking. I don't write that genre, remember?

Here are several easy swaps I now use for those overworked words:

Walk – rush, step, pace, cross, stride, amble, hike, march, stroll, and the rarely used sashay, saunter, frolic, or glide.

Look – Peer, study, glance, observe, watch, gaze, and stare.

Small – Tiny, miniature, little, miniscule, and insignificant. Now I'm laughing because I know you are too.

Study your work to find weak, repetitive verbs that you fall back on. Notice I didn't say look at your own work; I learned my lesson. Make a list of your well-meaning feeble verbs and include synonyms for easy reference. I used to keep a list like this by my computer. By now, I've learned to steer clear of boring, bland words. And by all means, use a thesaurus. There's one right on your laptop.

But, there's always a but, isn't there. It's fine to *occasionally* use a common word like walk, look, or small. We can't have our characters sashaying while peering over miniature menus all the time. That would be overkill. Isn't the English language fascinating? I love it.

DIALOGUE TAGS

Just a quick mention of dialogue tags. The majority of editors and publishing houses tell you to use "said." It's far less obtrusive and readers gloss over this dialogue tag. Of course, if the character is asking a question, you'll use "asked." I know. I know. It gets monotonous for us. Writers much prefer flowery words but you don't want to step on what your character is saying.

Also, when you only have two characters in a scene, after first making clear who is speaking, you can drop dialogue tags altogether. You probably don't even realize this when you're engrossed in a novel. You don't need to write "said" after every line of dialogue. It's clunky and unnecessary.

Here's an example:

Sipping a chilled chardonnay, Alex reached for Suzy's hand. "How are you handling the twins? Do you get any sleep?"

Suzy groaned as she pointed toward the dark circles under her eyes. "Take a guess."

"Sorry, Suzy Q. Wish I could help."

"I have a spare bedroom if you really want-"

A nervous giggle escaped as Alex took a bigger gulp. "Let's don't get carried away."

That's just a quick example off the top of my head. See where dialogue tags aren't needed after I first established the two friends, Alex and Suzy, were having a conversation? I wouldn't continue this way for an entire page or two without either adding an action or a dialogue tag occasionally. For instance, you can have a character reach for a purse, shove a hand in a pocket, glance at a cellphone, sneeze, wink, spill a drink, trip, or whatever action fits the scene. Just make sure it's obvious who is speaking so the reader doesn't get lost.

I'd say ninety-five percent of my dialogue tags include "said" or "asked." But, as with every rule in English, occasionally, a character really needs to whisper, hiss, or bellow, in my opinion. Just make sure these are used sparingly and avoid adverbs like the one I just used.

DO YOUR RESEARCH

Historical fiction writers are well known for doing extensive research. After all, they have to capture the era, clothing, automobiles, food, language, and more to set the tone. Research is crucial no matter what genre you're writing.

I assume memoir writers rely on journals, diaries, old letters, interactions with older relatives, and their own memory. Nonfiction writers also must do a great deal of research, often scientific or medical in nature, depending on the book.

As a contemporary romance and women's fiction novelist, I also have to conduct research. For my novels, I've researched:

✓ Moonshine
✓ Elvis (That was fun!)
✓ Talking parrots (Also enjoyable.)
✓ Tropical storms
✓ Boating terms
✓ Coast Guard lingo
✓ Bats
✓ Mullets
✓ 80s (The decade, attire, music, and slang.)
✓ VW Microbus
✓ Mood rings
✓ Wedding cake decorating
✓ DNA testing

And that's just for starters. You can likely tell by my research what some of my books are about. I've researched far more than this over the years. Research is extremely important to make your work realistic and compelling, plus your readers will appreciate the effort.

FINDING YOUR MOJO

Don't be dismayed if you lose your mojo or simply need a day or week off. If you feel blocked, it's better to go outside, watch a movie, take a walk, shop, walk on the beach, go boating, get a massage, grill a burger, sit at a coffee shop and absorb the atmosphere, hike the mountains, or a nature trail. Whatever you enjoy doing, do that thing—the one that makes you forget everything else.

If writing becomes a chore and a burden, it will show in your work. The encumbrance will be an unwanted strain. Your characters will become wooden. Your dialogue will be stilted. You'll get frown lines. You never want to push so hard that you begin to hate the work and want to throw your laptop across the room. It happens, but try to avoid these problematic feelings.

I know many authors who write seven days a week. I don't. People who have so-called "normal" jobs get time off. Writers need that as well, in my humble opinion. In fact, my cover artist has stopped working evenings and weekends. She doesn't even answer email until the following morning. I applaud this and think more of us need to follow her example. We all need to recharge our batteries. When you don't force it, I predict your muse will return in record time.

When I absolutely need to get a high word count for weeks in a row to meet a deadline, I pull out my favorite writerly mugs. One says, "Writing is my superpower. What's yours?" This one makes me smile and is motivational. I also have a sweatshirt that says: "Careful, or you'll end up in my novel." You've probably all seen that one. I can see you nodding in agreement.

Find what works for you, and enjoy the process, not to

mention this wonderful adventure called life.

WRITING TO MARKET

Writing to market means you're trying to hop on the newest trend. Remember when vampires were hot? And the *Fifty Shades of Grey* phenomenon? Many writers rolled up their sleeves and tried to jump on these bandwagons with a slew of vampire novels and hot, sexy novels flooding the already-burgeoning market.

The problem is, unless you can churn out several thousand words a day and can turn around a novel in three or four months, fully edited, the trend may be over before your book is published. The market might have moved on to mermaids and unicorns or leprechauns and werewolves. Sure, there will always be fans for these books, but unless you catch the wave and ride it while it's happening, you'll likely miss the trend.

A caveat: Maybe you love writing about vampires or super steamy novels. If you do, you should. This may sound like I'm talking out of both sides of my mouth, but I'm saying write about what interests you. Decide what your passion is and what will keep you coming back to the keyboard. Day after day. Decide what topics make your mind soar and fingers fly across the keyboard. That's what you should write. If you force yourself to pen a genre that doesn't interest you, your writing will be dull, you won't want to work on your project, and worse, your readers will be bored and might never buy another one of your books.

Write what you know is a familiar mantra, especially for new authors. It is repeated at workshop after workshop, undoubtedly for good reason. What we know is familiar territory and interests us. That means our work will come across as realistic, intriguing, and compelling. Who can argue with that logic?

USING MONIKERS & PEN NAMES

Writers call themselves by many monikers: author, aspiring writer, budding writer, unpublished writer, newbie writer, or simply writer, among others. I often see the debate online whether to use writer versus author. To me, if you're published, whether traditionally or indie, with your name splashed big and bold across the front of a shiny book, you're an author. If you're still submitting your manuscript or haven't yet indie published, you're a writer. But that's my opinion. I say call yourself whatever name motivates you to finish your book.

As far as pen names, many authors prefer the anonymity for numerous reasons. Some may be attorneys, doctors, or teachers who write steamy romances. I actually know several who do exactly that and they don't want their employers to know. Using a pen name is entirely up to you and will likely depend on your genre, profession, and preference.

I do not use a pen name, however, if I wrote erotica, I would. Why? Because I also write children's books. It wouldn't be the best combo and would confuse my brand, not to mention my readers. I have many author friends who write in this genre and are quite successful. Romance is a billion-dollar industry, which is inspiring. Who doesn't love a happy ending?

Here's a funny story about a Florida art gallery I approached to carry my books. During the interview, I sat across from the artist in charge of visiting artists. She was sweet and kind. But before we discussed whether the gallery would carry my work, she plucked out at least five typewritten pages of printed book covers by another Beth Carter. You see, her books are racy and the gallery was not going to have any of that, saying it would upset their clientele. I glanced at the book covers and said they weren't mine. But the artist insisted on pointing to every single cover, one by one, and asking if it was mine. I noted that the other prolific Beth Carter uses her middle initial. I don't, plus our initials are different. I actually pulled out my driver's license to prove my identity.

My point is I didn't get huffy, and my relationship with the gallery and the interviewer turned out to be a wonderful experience. To this day, I'm friends with that artist and many others from the gallery, which showcased my novels and children's books for years. They even hosted me for several book signings. Bottom line: Always be professional in this business.

Back to pen names. Another reason I don't use one is because it's too much work. I'd need double the amount of social media pages—one for my personal accounts and one for my pen name. I'm simply too lazy to have separate Facebook, Twitter, Instagram, Pinterest, Goodreads, and a website for basically two people. But, hey, if you have the gumption and time, go for it.

JOIN LOCAL & ONLINE WRITING GROUPS

Hopefully, you're already a member of local, national, and online writing groups. I'm a member of several online groups and used to belong to three local writing groups. Happily, they were coordinated on different Saturdays of each month. The romance group met the first Saturday; the mystery writers met the second Saturday; and a multi-genre group met the third Saturday, but only quarterly. During the summer lake season, three meetings per month is quite a commitment. But I gleaned a great deal from the speakers and attended most of the meetings where I also spoke on occasion.

We had presentations from attorneys, police officers, a sheriff, a prison guard, a forensic specialist, paranormal ghost watchers—for real—and many more. Writers also spoke about their areas of expertise, whether it was dialogue, plotting, humor, writing a series, marketing, or other topics. Some spoke about hobbies or pastimes, which is great for character development. Honestly, it only takes a few words or sentences for writers to get an idea. Sometimes I would barely make it to my car before jotting down notes for my novel. Occasionally, I'd pull into a Starbucks, laptop in tow, and bang out several thousand words.

Join as many local writing groups as you can. You will appreciate being around fellow writers. You'll hold one another accountable, have critiques, and sometimes the entire meeting would be a write-in, which was also great fun. Google groups in your genre of choice, and don't be afraid to mix it up like I did by going to one meeting for romance authors and another for mystery/thriller writers. They will both offer varying facets that will bolster your storyline. If you don't find a meeting in your area, start one. Fellow writers understand one another and are a supportive bunch. Bonus: When you do have a book signing, these folks will be the first in line to buy your book—behind your mom, of course.

BE A HEALTHY WRITER

Writers sit far too much. It's what we do. It's unhealthy, plus weight gain is inevitable. Far more important than weight gain is our health, which goes hand in hand. Doctors always talk about the importance of walking, but it's difficult to write while walking. I get it. Writing is a sedentary career choice. However, you *can* dictate. I know some authors who dictate entire books. I wish I could. I've only used dictation once, and it doesn't come naturally to me.

Another option is standing desks. I bought one six months ago. Guess what? It's still in the box. I've tried placing my laptop on a higher counter so I can stand, but the counter isn't wide enough, plus I prefer using a separate keyboard and mouse. I always end up back at the kitchen table or at a coffee shop.

To make myself move, I set a timer on the microwave. You could also ask Alexa to remind you or set a timer on your cellphone. I've found I need to get up every thirty-five minutes. Not every thirty-six minutes or every thirty-four. It's a pretty exact science with me. When the timer goes off, I make myself stretch, march in place, walk from one end of the house to the other a couple of times, or occasionally go up and down the stairs. I also hydrate and eat a healthy snack like almonds. Of course, like most writers, I mainline coffee.

My husband says I look like Ichabod Crane when I write since I get involved in my story and am hunched over my keyboard. Um, that's not the best image and I certainly don't want to create a hump on my back, so I bought a riser for my laptop. It's only four inches high and cost about twenty dollars at an office supply store. It has helped my posture immensely. I still get lazy and hunch over, but I really do try to work on my posture. Oh, the timer just went off. I'll be back in a few minutes.

AVOID POLITICS & RELIGION

This is entirely up to you, of course, but I've seen high-profile, extremely successful authors go on and on about politics online. Curious, I read the comments on social media and couldn't believe how many readers said they'd never buy that author's books again. This person has so many sales, that those particular readers might not be missed, but if you're just starting out or are a midlist author, you can't afford to turn readers away. Why chance it? Talk to your friends or family instead. Get it off your chest without possibly losing half your readership.

To emphasize this point, ask yourself if you like it when musicians or actors discuss politics, especially daily and with a loud megaphone. I generally don't, and I'm an independent. I've voted for both sides of the political aisle over the decades. I'd rather be entertained and I bet the majority of people feel the same way about every type of artist.

When I worked in banking, my boss, the bank president, was a staunch conservative. He didn't even like cursing. I hope he hasn't read my novels that have a few f-bombs. That's our secret. To reiterate my point about readers getting offended, I remember going to work one Monday after the Grammy Awards. My boss, who is a great guy, by the way, and introduced me to my husband, told me he was highly offended that Garth Brooks, an entertainer he enjoyed, had used the word "damn" in his winning speech. That's my point. People are easily offended, so why chance throwing politics and religion into the mix. I do think some characters should curse, though. That's real life. A cop is not going to be on a foot chase and yell, "Crap. Darn it. The meth dealer got away." There would be a plethora of cussing afterward.

Remember, writing is a business. The last thing you want to do—especially in the early years—is turn off potential readers. Why risk destroying your career over a two-sentence tweet?

WRITING SHORTCUTS

I mentioned I wrote *The Quarantine Cookbook* during the horrific 2020 pandemic. What I haven't said is I wrote it in *thirteen* days. I couldn't believe it because I included almost 200 recipes, indexed by section, from Appetizers, Sides, Soups, Entrees, Meatless Meals, to Desserts. Additionally, I included sections on Non-Stir Crazy Activities and Six-Word Memoirs on Quarantine Life.

How did I write a 227-page book in less than two weeks? I discovered the wonder of that little microphone in Word. And, my word, is it ever a time saver! Try it. I know authors who have carpel tunnel—so do I—and they dictate most if not all of their novels. I haven't quite gotten to that point.

Another favorite tool is the yellow highlighter. I use it to highlight each chapter heading. I mention the character and main plot point of the chapter. That way, when I'm editing and moving chapters around, I immediately know who the POV character is and what the scene is about. This is, by far, my favorite writing tool. I know many writers use sophisticated software, pin scenes or chapters to boards and copy and paste them later, but this simple method works for me.

I also have a small heart-shaped silicone wrist rest that sits in front of my mouse. This helps prevent carpel tunnel. When I'm closing in on an 80,000-word manuscript, I'm often, sadly, in wrist braces from my years of extreme amounts of typing.

STUDY CRAFT BOOKS ON WRITING

I'm thrilled you're reading my craft book on writing, which also covers inspiration, websites, marketing, grammar/punctuation, pitching to agents, and more. There are many varied craft books on writing. Some discuss characters, others focus on dialogue or plot. There are even books on how to infuse humor, however, I think you're either funny or you're not. A few suggest how to write faster, while many focus on marketing.

Seek out books where you feel you need guidance. Is your dialogue stilted or do you have difficulty coming up with unique characters or careers? Is plot an issue? Do you use the same actions over and over? In my first novel, my characters seemed to blow out their breath often. They must have been light headed and were clearly quite exasperated.

You'll find a plethora of books covering each of these subjects. Barnes & Noble has an excellent reference section for writers. I go in spurts and read craft books in between writing and reading novels. I enjoy having them on my bookshelf for quick reference, even if I haven't had time to read half of the books I own. It's important to educate yourself and focus on any weak spots. I also love reading quotes for inspiration, especially those by famous authors, as you'll notice throughout this book.

Some of my favorite craft books to date are: *How I Write. Secrets of A Bestselling Author* by Janet Evanovich and Ina Yalof, which has been out for over a decade. Janet really kicks you in the butt and takes a no-excuses attitude. I needed that book in the early years of my career.

I purchased a series of craft books from Angela Ackerman & Becca Puglisi, including *The Emotion Thesaurus: A Writer's Guide to Character Expression*, as well as many others by these authors, who have created a much-needed niche in writing guides for every possible scenario. Andrew Mayne's *How to Write A Novella in 24 Hours* was interesting, though, I really didn't learn how to accomplish that feat. Still, I was fascinated by his profession as a magician, likely since my daughter worked with several magicians as an assistant for years, performing several times at The Magic Castle in Los Angeles and overseas in New Zealand. She still won't tell me how they sawed her in half or locked her in a cage and fifteen seconds later she was at the back of the theater in an entirely different outfit. It kind of drives me nuts, but she's sticking to the confidentiality contract the magicians made her sign. Good for her, even though, I promised not to tell.

I'm currently reading Jennifer Probst's book, *Write Naked, A Bestseller's Secrets to Writing Romance*. I even bought the accompanying pink tee shirt, which I wear while writing (not naked.)

I really enjoyed *2,000 to 10,000* by Rachel Aaron, which is about so much more than writing fast, though she provides interesting tips to improve your speed. I loved Aaron's three-step process for creating a character ARC and conflict. It's absolutely perfect.

Two of the most well-known, incredible books for writers are *On Writing* by Stephen King and *Bird by Bird* by Anne Lamott. Joanna Penn has penned (like what I did there?!) a number of books for authors. I've recently discovered the entertaining author David Gaughran and purchased his book, *Let's Get Digital*. I knew I'd like his book the minute he mentioned moving to a fishing village in Portugal, which didn't improve his time outside. I laughed out loud. Every writer can relate. I'd love to know what's on your shelf or nightstand!

I Wrote A Book. Now What?

In addition to witty, helpful books on writing, don't forget to subscribe to writerly magazines. I love *Writer's Digest* and *The Writer*. There are also regional magazines and those by genre. For instance, poets have their own magazine, as do mystery writers. The largest writing organization in the world, Romance Writers of America, has a monthly publication for members called *Romance Writers Report*. Always stay informed, whether you prefer to read online or are old school like me and wish to hold a book or magazine.

READ

It's important for writers to take time to read. Most authors have been avid readers since they were kids. I was. My favorite childhood books were *Charlotte's Web*, *The Boxcar Children*, and the *Little House on the Prairie* series. Think about the books that have stuck with you since childhood as inspiration and motivation to create your best work.

We didn't have a lot of money growing up, and I loved going to the library monthly and getting an armload of books. When a bookmobile starting coming around our neighborhood, it was better than the ice cream truck. Okay, it was equally as good. Even though I played outside, rode my bike, and enjoyed sports, I was also perfectly happy in my room getting lost in other worlds.

We all want to create literary wonder, provide escapism, or teach about a product or service. Writers have endless imaginations that we want to share with the world. It's a special gift. Embrace it.

If you're stuck on a scene, read. Many say to read in the genre in which you write. I disagree. I read many genres. In fact, even though I've never penned a thriller or a psychological suspense, those are my favorite books to read. I often say thrillers have taught me more about pacing than any college writing class. Ditto for teaching me the importance of cliffhangers. I also enjoy mysteries, romance, women's fiction, memoirs, and biographies. And cookbooks. I have a gazillion and finally wrote one during the pandemic.

Take a break, treat yourself, and read. Reading is the kind of homework everyone enjoys, especially writers since we know the amount of work that goes into every book.

INSPIRATION

"You might be poor, your shoes might be broken, but your mind is a palace." ~Frank McCourt

FINDING INSPIRATION

Let's face it. We all have times when the words don't flow. When I get in this non-wordsmithery funkity funk, I step away from my laptop and do something entirely different to mix it up. I might go outside since most writers are practically recluses. My favorite non-writing activities include shopping, boating, board games, going for a drive, listening to country or rock music, visiting friends and relatives, and probably more shopping. T. J. Maxx misses me when I'm on a deadline. Inspiration comes in many forms. Here are some of my favorites.

Ripped From the Headlines

I've gotten a few story ideas from news stories or articles I've read in newspapers or magazines. Of course, I change it completely—such as the main character's sex, career, where they live, quirks, hobbies, and so on. It's fun to think of a different outcome and make a true story fictional.

One recurring theme that often occurs during the holidays is about a kind-hearted secret Santa who pays for strangers' layaway purchases. Usually this is done anonymously at a big box store. One year after hearing about such kindness, I was inspired to write *Miracle On Aisle Two,* where a single mom is fired two weeks before Christmas and is distraught in the layaway aisle of Target since she can no longer afford her young daughter's toys. Enter generous, handsome stranger.

Eavesdrop

I'm serious. You will inevitably hear juicy dialogue that you can use in your next book. Writers are famous for eavesdropping, so if you're sitting beside someone with a laptop, don't tell your most inner secrets. I heard a great story in a hotel lobby once and could barely eat my breakfast because I kept surreptitiously typing notes to myself via email. I haven't yet written that book but will someday. I recommend changing the names, locations, and genders to protect the innocent.

Childhood Memories

For my award-winning *Coconuts* series, I was inspired by hippies since I'm a 70s girl. I loved reliving the music, tie-dye, and peace signs, and happily included this fun, crazy era in my novels. And who doesn't love researching mood rings, a VW Microbus, and bellbottoms? Some of that bled into the 80s, another fun decade.

If I ever write about a teen who needs a job, I might have her work in a movie theater like I did during high school. The smell of salty popcorn still brings back fond memories. I made $1.10 per hour, which I was thrilled to get since I only wanted enough money to buy gasoline and cute clothes. My boss, the kind manager, hired me at age fifteen and told me to tell everyone I was sixteen, which I happily did since we didn't have much money growing up and I needed the cash.

While working the concession stand, I learned to add quickly in my head. Most items were twenty-five, fifty or seventy-five cents, so it was pretty easy. Once, when I had a huge order for a midnight movie, I calculated the order in my head as I filled multiple red and white containers of popcorn, cups of soda, one-third the size we have now, and squirted mustard on a few hot dogs. I'll never forget the big, burly man's squinted eyes as he challenged the total, which was over nine dollars. Quite a lot back then. He said, "How do you know?" I pointed to my head, as in I was smart, but grabbed a napkin, scribbled down the order, and proved my math skills which, thank goodness, equaled my original calculation. I could tell he was disappointed.

I have many childhood memories I've incorporated in my *Coconuts* series, especially in my novel, *Cowboys At Coconuts*, which involves a cowboy and a socialite. The cowboy encourages the New Yorker to enjoy the simpler things in life as he teaches her how to skip rocks, hunt for arrowheads, and pitch a tent. My dad and I have done all of those things many times, and it was a thrill to tap into those fond memories. I also remember the gorgeous, fragrant lilac bush in our back yard and watching Mom place several lilacs in a vase on the kitchen table. My sister and I would suck honeysuckle that trailed over a fading, gray fence between the neighbor's house and our driveway. Have fun tapping into your own memories. They're sure to enrich your writing.

Professions

When my daughter was planning her wedding, I observed a harried wedding planner, clipboard in hand, and immediately decided one of my main characters would be a wedding planner. Over-the-top neurotic brides and their mothers and mothers-in-law have become lively, unpredictable characters. Whether they're a main character or a secondary character, your readers will likely relate to their antics.

I also drew on my personal experience as a bank marketer who dated a cop. Everyone tells me I'm one of my main characters, Alex (for Alexandra) who also happens to be a banker and dates a cop. Hmm. They may have a point.

Weather

In *Chaos At Coconuts*, I paid homage to the horrific Joplin EF5 tornado from a decade ago. That tragedy inspired several heartbreaking, albeit touching, tornado scenes. It was a great way for the students at Hilltop High School, where one of my main characters is a guidance counselor, to bring the popular and not-so-popular kids together for one heroic mission.

As avid boaters, we've also gotten caught in several bad storms, a few where I didn't think we'd make it back to shore. During the time, I certainly wasn't thinking the tropical storm would make a great boating scene in a future novel, but once I got my land legs back, it did inspire me to add a scary boating scene in my novel *Sleeping With Elvis*.

Travel

Travel is always inspirational, whether you're a writer or not. Your writing will be richer when you can name actual landmarks, restaurants, streets, smells, food, dress, music, and generally, the local flavor. I've created scenes in Paris, New York City, Nashville, Hollywood, and Florida, all places I've been. Travel is a heady experience. When you can bring it to life for readers, they won't be able to put your book down.

Study People

A unique, young Goth—is that word still in vogue?— couple at a local burger joint inspired the couple for my Halloween wedding in *Chaos At Coconuts*. I study people at restaurants, the pharmacy, hair salons, Starbucks, parks, and grocery stores. Not in a weird, stalkerish way, of course. Just for research. Look around and pay attention in this hectic world. Potential characters are all around you. Observation skills are crucial for a writer.

In fact, after attending two Elvis tribute concerts, the artist, Chris MacDonald, inspired my main character, Ty Townsend, who is an Elvis impersonator. Chris looks exactly like a young Elvis and he's extremely gracious in his tributes to the King. As I stood in line after the concert, you should have seen the look on the entertainer's face when I told him he was the inspiration for the hero in my novel. After he read the title, *Sleeping With Elvis*, he grinned and asked, "Was I good?" He autographed a DVD of his live show, while I autographed my book. We took photos and he promised to read my book on his tour bus. See, you never know who will inspire you!

Music

As mentioned under a "Writing Advice" section, I use music often to set the tone for scenes in my novels. For inspiration, I often turn to country music. After all, country songs are almost always relatable. They remind us of bygone eras sitting on a porch listening to parents and grandparents weave tales. Sure, many of the visuals are country roads, girls, whiskey, and pickup trucks, but they generally tell a charming story. Listen to the lyrics. Even if you don't become inspired, I bet you'll be tapping your foot and have a smile on your face.

Reading

Most writers are avid readers. When I'm on a deadline, occasionally I won't read for weeks, which has an adverse effect—I almost always get stuck in a writing rut. Once I realize this, I pick up a novel and the juices flow again. I think it has to do with seeing how easy the finished product appears, though, we all know it's anything but, plus the pure joy of getting lost in a story will have me tapping away on my keyboard in no time.

Words

Writers love words. We adore them. We can't get enough of them. I can see one word and my imagination will run wild. Actually, I read a particular word in a magazine article, and it's going to be the impetus for my next novel. It'll actually be in the title. I'm chomping at the bit to write that book. When I spotted this seemingly innocuous word in a writing magazine, I scribbled all over the page, in between paragraphs, and in every margin. Imagine how one common word can spark an entire novel. I'm not trying to be mysterious about the word I fell in love with, but I always have cover reveals, so I can't tell you since it's going to be in a future title. Watch my website and blog for updates.

Find a word that charges your imagination. Open a dictionary or thesaurus, flip through a few pages, point, and challenge yourself to use that particular word in your book. Better yet, play Scrabble and dare yourself to use one or more obscure words in your work. Bonus: It'll force you out of your writer's cave for an afternoon.

In the next section, I share exercises from my super creative college lit professor. By tapping into your senses, you'll be able to create relatable, realistic characters and powerful, compelling stories.

OBSERVATION EXERCISE TO SHARPEN YOUR SENSES

I attended evening college while working full time at a private college during the day. After hearing my uncle, an English professor, Wayne Holmes, explain tuition remission and how his four kids were able to attend college for free, I set out to make sure I got a job at that university. I never could have afforded it, otherwise. On Sundays, I always filled a coffee cup, curled up on the couch, and scanned the want ads. This was in the mid-eighties and before email. I noticed an ad in the newspaper for an executive secretary for the college president. I was thrilled since I had excellent secretarial skills and had even competed in typing and shorthand competitions in high school. This was right up my alley and I requested an interview the following morning.

Driving around Drury Lane, I wondered where to park when I found Burnham Hall, the building where the President's Office was. As I approached the stairs, several students swarmed by, chatting in an easy manner. Campus life, akin to a small-town community, was exactly what I needed and came at the perfect time of my life—during an unexpected divorce when my daughter was barely two. I could tell the president, Dr. Moore, liked me and approved of my resume and skills. He really liked the fact that I knew shorthand and said that would be key for taking the minutes of board meetings. But he hesitated and admitted he feared since I was going through a divorce that I wouldn't be able to focus on my job. I forced a smile and convinced him I needed something else to focus on and was eager to work. Besides, I was already eyeing that big desk in the spacious outer office. Okay, I didn't mention that part. Needless to say, I got the job and stayed in that position for seven years, mainly because I wanted to get a degree. The president kept promising to promote me—after I got a degree—saying he wanted to groom me for a development position, meaning call on potential donors. I wasn't the least bit interested in that job but I adored interacting with the faculty, staff, students, and the trustees. It was a well-rounded position, which left me with fond memories and many long-time friends.

Evening college was tough but fun. I loved my writing classes, but for some reason, chose to major in business. As a single mom, I needed a steady paycheck and benefits. Evening students were all ages and from every walk of life. One white-haired, eighty-something woman was in my algebra class. I always wondered why she'd put herself through that agony at her advanced age, but at the same time, I deeply admired her. So I'd only miss one night with my daughter, I routinely scheduled two classes on the same evening. One course was from 5:20 p.m. until 8 p.m. and the second class began at 8:10 until 10:50 p.m. What a grueling schedule, especially since I had a toddler in tow. Thankfully, my mother-in-law lived nearby and babysat. Don't ask me how I survived the semester when I took economics and statistics on the same Monday night. I'm sure I was in a foul mood the entire four months.

My favorite semesters were when I took writing classes. After one particular creative writing class, I told my English professor, Jo Van Arkel, that she could inspire a rock. She was adept at finding unique ways for her students to tap into their creativity. Once she assigned an observation exercise, which became one of my favorite writing activities.

The instructor told us to choose a place, any place, inside or out. This was before cellphones, so I wasn't the least bit distracted. I decided to go to a bus stop near a downtown movie theater where I worked as a teen. Armed with a yellow legal pad and pen, I adhered to the professor's instructions to use all my senses. What followed was the smell of popcorn from the theater, chatter from passersby, horns blaring, and exhaust fumes from nearby cars. The concrete bench was cold and hard. My hair became tangled from the wind. Eventually, a couple joined me inside the bus stop and began chatting with one another. I don't remember their conversation but do remember I was happy I still remembered shorthand and got their conversation down almost verbatim. I remember typing a four- or five-page essay of my experience. My instructor was pleased, gave me an A, and said, "So, a story evolved, eh?"

The entire purpose of this unique exercise was to impress on the students the importance of bringing stories to life using our senses—sight, smell, hear, taste, and touch. It's truly magical when you incorporate the senses in your writing. Make sure your characters feel, see, smell, hear, and touch whatever the scene requires.

Even if I look ridiculous, I occasionally act out a scene to try and figure out how a hand motion would be conveyed or how a character's face might scrunch up at the scent of a steaming pile of cow crap. This is easier to do at home than in public, but I've done it in coffee shops as well. Most know I'm an author and expect this type of behavior. It's part of the job.

I encourage you to try my professor's observation exercise. It's one of my favorites. Pick an intriguing spot, get comfy, take coffee or water, something to write with, and begin.

DIAGRAM YOUR CHILDHOOD HOME

This same college professor gave us another interesting exercise. She asked us to take out a piece of paper and draw the inside of our childhood home. I started with the living room, added the kitchen, two bedrooms, and one bathroom. I grew up in a tiny home—before they were trendy. As I stared at the diagram of our house, childhood memories filled my adult mind. I remembered sharing my bedroom with my sister, hearing my parents' whisper and giggle in bed, watching a black and white television and adjusting the foil-covered rabbit ears. Sounds of the neighbor kids' happy shrieks filled the room through our open screen door.

We didn't have much money and neither did our neighbors, so we all crowded around our new television in our modest living room. We were the talk of the neighborhood, I'm sure. Staring at the diagram, I remembered when we covered our hardwood floors with an emerald green carpet and how my parent's sophisticated friend said it looked "lush."

Mom's cooking came flooding back, and I could visualize a big pot of brown beans simmering on the stove with golden cornbread in the oven, while Dad read the newspaper from cover to cover. Weekends were filled with visits from relatives, Hide 'n Seek, and our parents playing Rook, a rambunctious—according to their giggles, snorts, and jokes—card game. I always made extra trips to the kitchen to get water, just so I could see what was so intriguing about those cards. When I grew up, I definitely wanted to play cards, drink beer, and smoke cigarettes just like them. That didn't happen, but it was a happy, fun-loving household and a great time to grow up.

Occasionally, we made homemade ice cream, always vanilla, with the occasional bits of banana or peach, which were both a treat. Thoughts of sitting on top of the cold, hard crank while everyone took turns churning the icy dessert made me smile. On the porch, red roses grew up the trellis, and Dad taught me how to ride a bike in the church yard across the street. I still sucked my thumb at age five, and the used bike, which Dad painted a glittery lime green, complete with streamers and a white banana seat, was my reward if I'd stop the thumb sucking. I did. Mostly.

During wintertime, he often pulled my sister and me down the alley on a sled when it snowed, much to our delight. Dad and I played catch for practice when I was on a softball team and Mom made most of my clothes, even tiny clothes for my Barbies. I'd give anything to still have the gorgeous black velvet gown she made for Barbie. The sewing machine was nearly always out. She even made my homecoming dress when I was up for Homecoming Queen (I lost by two votes according to the student senate president, not that I remember that minor, heartbreaking detail after many decades.) But—cough—that fact did make it into one of the final scenes in *Thursdays At Coconuts*, which was a satisfying chapter. What can I say? Losing by two votes stung like a two-star review.

As I stared at the diagram and our floorplan, it was amazing how all these memories rushed back. I encourage you to try this exercise. You'll be certain to be inspired whether you're writing a memoir or simply need to add more detail to your work in progress. And your floorplan doesn't have to look like an architectural masterpiece. I can barely draw anything besides flowers and stick people. Just make squares of each room as they appeared in your home and label the rooms. Sit back, study your childhood home, and memories will pour in, I promise.

HOW TRADITIONAL JOBS ENRICHED MY WRITING

Instead of a midlife crisis with a shiny convertible, I reinvented myself as a writer. At a certain age, okay, at fifty, I reassessed my corporate career and forty-plus-hour work week. As a single mom, I had worked in education, banking, and healthcare. The first was as an administrative assistant, until I attended evening college while working full-time and obtained a business degree. Afterward, I spent nearly twenty years working in marketing in three industries: healthcare, banking, and green heat. Let me tell you, marketing is marketing, no matter what the industry. And that background has been a huge gift while promoting my books.

Working outside the home in different environments enriches our writing by providing needed background on the type of businesses, employees, boards, organizational flow, business issues, colleagues, competition, business layout, and much more depending on your career choice.

Environments also stimulate our senses. Think of the antiseptic smell that hits you in the face the moment you step inside a hospital. Imagine working there while pregnant with morning sickness. Yep. I did that. Now, wouldn't that make for a great character? I plan to write that novel someday. I also witnessed doctors with egos bigger than a mall, as well as the caring touch of nurses.

People act differently no matter where they work and this enables writers to create the perfect character. Consider the buttoned-up corporate type versus the always-badly-dressed college professor, usually with white socks and sandals or a mismatched plaid and floral outfit. Yes, I'm stereotyping, but

I stared at these wonderful, intelligent academics who happily—and likely purposely—disregarded the latest fashion whims for decades, so I'm allowed.

Realize dialogue will be much different in a hospital setting than a bank or a construction zone, for instance. Consider hearing "STAT" in overhead announcements every few minutes versus a quiet bank lobby. Consider crouching and getting cramps while on deployment if you're writing a memoir about military life, or a novel with a military character. Remember David Bloom, the fabulous journalist with NBC, who was embedded with the military? He got DVT from crouching while they were on missions and it killed him. It was shocking, sad, and probably taught us all a term, Deep Vein Thrombosis, that most of us had never heard. Do that in your writing. Details like this enrich your work and make the reading educational and compelling.

One of the characters in my *Coconuts* series, Alex, short for Alexandra, is a bank marketer. Guess what? So was I. She also dates a cop and—ditto, like I mentioned previously. I also plan to have a novel set on a college campus and in a hospital. Since I worked in both industries for years, I'll be able to write about nuances between employees, administration, physicians, professors, staff, students, and board members that I'd never find while Googling these professions. Research is your friend, but it's hard to beat real-life experiences.

Think about where you, your partner, and family members work. I'm sure you can find a plethora of plots, setting, and character ideas to ensure authentic writing. Whether you're a car mechanic, dentist, nanny, dog walker, hair stylist, or whatever your profession, tap into the unlimited possibilities of each career and bring your characters to life.

Even if you don't love punching a clock, embrace the fact that you'll be able to turn your long days into rich book details. That's some satisfaction, right?

TAP INTO PASTIMES & HOBBIES FOR IDEAS

If you've never worked outside the home, don't worry. I'm sure you have hobbies and plenty of interests you can apply to your writing. For example, I've taken classes in floral arranging, painting, candle wicking—that doesn't have anything to do with candles, by the way—piano, cooking, boating, and speleology, which helped with an outdoor Halloween wedding scene in *Chaos At Coconuts*. Just imagine the variety of characters I could come up with if each one were proficient in just one of these specialties.

Make a list of classes you've taken, hobbies, pastimes, and passions. Think all the way back to high school. I bet you'll be surprised by all the knowledge you have. Maybe you worked at a movie theater like me as a teen and are able to convey the smell and taste of salty popcorn, the crowd rush before the movie and during intermission, juggling giant cups of soda without spilling it on yourself or customers, and the long lines of patrons clamoring to see the newest release.

Likewise, write down the places you've worked since high school. You'll be surprised how each of these will spark imaginative ideas in your writing. Hmm. Now I want to take another craft class or find a piano teacher who won't give seven songs to learn weekly. That was stressful. When you reflect on your own pastimes, besides being an enjoyable trip down memory lane, you'll surely think of unique characters or plot ideas.

LEAVE THE HOUSE

Writers are an interesting bunch. I can say that since I am one. I get lost in my fictional world—or nonfictional kingdom—on occasion and tend to let things fall apart around me. Clutter piles up, dirty clothes spill out of hampers, notes overrun every counter, and I suggest eating out to my husband. Yes, *again.* Sometimes, I even forget to wash my hair. Every writer I know does this because we don't want to leave the world we've created. The words are flowing. But guess what? It's important to occasionally step away from the keyboard.

Of course, this advice makes more sense when there isn't a worldwide pandemic, but let's all cross our fingers and toes and hope we're set free soon. Here are a few observations I noticed when I left my house:

✓ At a restaurant, a patron looked exactly like a character I pictured for one of my children's picture books. In fact, I had to circle the room twice to get a good look. I fought the urge to take a photo, which wasn't easy.

✓ At a car wash, a man at the cash register was the inspiration for a fictional professor on a college campus, down to his attire and gray ponytail.

✓ My husband and I overheard a pathetic conversation at a pizza parlor. I took out paper and pen and began making notes. The guy was desperate to get his date to go on a trip with him, but the more he talked, the more she stared at her phone, totally uninterested. Undeterred, he practically pleaded with her, saying he'd pay for everything and they could have separate hotel rooms. Her response: "I'm having a party that weekend." His response: "Can I come?"

Oh, my God. I couldn't write fast enough and my spouse, who feared they'd catch on to my eavesdropping, began shouting, "Coffee. Bread. We need milk too." It was both hilarious and sad. I wouldn't enjoy creating the guy's character unless I gave him a backbone toward the end. Her totally disinterested character, on the other hand, would be fun to write.

These are just a few examples of why we need to go out in public. A nature walk will add to your writing because you'll utilize your senses and possibly incorporate unique trees, flowers, or even animals into your work. I have a crazy cursing parrot in my novel, *Sleeping With Elvis.* Everyone loves that parrot and so do I.

Even if you don't overhear a crazy conversation, you'll get some much-needed exercise and vitamin D. Have you seen the meme showing tan lines for different professions? The writer is the only one without a tan. Hilarious and true.

SOAK UP THE SCENERY

Soaking up your surroundings, underscores the importance of leaving the house. When you are able to take a real vacation (hello, pandemic from hell), focus on every detail. You'll not only relax but you will unknowingly—or possibly knowingly—gather ideas for future books.

Pay attention to every detail—the hotel, resort, campground, RV, airplane, helicopter, car, or whatever your mode of travel and destination. Consider how it smells. Do you smell the infamous Kansas City barbecue? Or mouthwatering pizza in Italy? Maybe a lilac bush reminds you of your grandmother. Really concentrate on your surroundings.

Also consider what you hear. Maybe it's country music blaring from the honky tonks that line Nashville's Broadway Street. If jazz fills the air, you might be in New Orleans, or a steel drum could mean Jamaica, one of my favorite destinations.

Are kids squealing and splashing in the ocean or the lake? Do you see teens in bikinis and colorful swim trunks playing volleyball on the beach? Maybe you spot a dog wading up to its neck at the lake and repetitively jumping off a dock, or see jet skiers as you notice rays of sun bounce off the water like diamonds. At a Happy Hour place, you'd probably hear entertaining dialogue that could be used in books. All you have to do is be observant while you're taking time off.

Treat yourself to a long-overdue massage and focus on the scent of lavender or eucalyptus filling the air. Be sure to include these details to make your characters jump off the page. Once, my husband got a massage and drooled on the poor masseur's pristine, white tennis shoes. I've never been that relaxed in my life, even after two glasses of wine or Xanax. But wouldn't that be a funny scene? Not in real life maybe, but on paper, heck yes. Speaking of, I would love a massage about now.

Another way to enrich your writing is to make a list of places you've been. Even if you've never left your hometown, you'll still find book fodder at a local barber shop, diner, church, or the town square. By making a list, you'll recount memories. I love to travel and have been to several states, islands, and countries including Italy, France, Greece, Mexico, Bahamas, Jamaica, Canada, and Monaco. Wow. If I set a novel in each of those places, look how many I would have. Of course, this travel was over a span of decades.

And shockingly—or not—you may not enjoy travel or be unable to leave your home. I have family members who don't like to travel unless it's across town to their favorite restaurant. But you can still have an adventure. Pitch a tent in the backyard, pop popcorn and have a movie marathon, or plan a board game competition among friends. Barbecuing in the back yard is always relaxing and delicious. Simply going on a nature walk will clear your mind and spark story ideas.

All of these details will enrich your writing. Going somewhere new and different will provide endless settings, dialogue, characterization, and plot and will enable you to create realistic characters. If you're writing nonfiction, these suggestions still apply. No one wants to read a dry book, no matter the genre.

USE UNIQUE WORDS

In my novels, I purposely set out to use new and unique words in each one. It's fun for me, as well as the reader, plus an uncommon word almost always inspires a scene. Here are a few that I've used as a character descriptor, to enhance the setting, or for dialogue:

Bamboozle	Skedaddle
Moonshine	Hullabaloo
Mullet	Skinny dipping
Gnarly	Paparazzi
Agog	Elvis impersonator
Chopper	Soliloquy
Serendipity	Hubbub
Burgeoning	Couture
Tornado/twister	Hoedown
Winter wonderland	Bohemian
Whimsical	VW Microbus
Mood ring	Tie dye
Bats—That's not a unique	
word but is a distinctive animal.	

I could continue into next week, but you already get a feel for some of my novels, don't you? Think of words that will make your work stand out and be unique.

WEBSITE TIPS

CLAIM YOUR NAME

If you don't do anything else I've recommended, please do this: Claim your name! This is of utmost importance when beginning your website search. Thankfully, as a newbie author, it occurred to me to Google Beth Carter. Guess what? There are two other women with my name who are authors. *Two.* What an eyebrow-raising coincidence. There are also sculptors, photographers, and artists with the same name; Beth Carter is obviously the name for many creatives. Wow.

My heart pounded as I quickly emailed a search engine to see if bethcarter.com was available, and eureka, it was. I bought bethcarter.com, bethcarter.net, and bethcarter.org. I also paid to secure this ten years out because I'm too afraid of losing my domain name. It's that important.

Google yourself right now to see if anyone else has claimed your name. Be sure to come back. What did you find? Are there other people with your name? Are they in the same industry? Claiming your public persona is more important than querying or perfecting your manuscript. That can all wait a day or three. Your online presence can't be messed with. If your name is available, make yourself a big note to get on this and contact trusted sites to host your website. Compare prices, ask around to see who others use, check their reviews, and secure your name/website. Whew. That was close.

Along this vein, some authors take out cutesy names or use the title of their book as their website. This isn't a great idea. People will likely remember your name but not the title of your book, plus you're going to write more than one book, right?

WEBSITE SUGGESTIONS

If you're tech savvy, unlike me, you may be able to create your own website. I do not possess that talent and hired an author friend who is an artist and a whiz with computers. First, I researched a gazillion author websites, decided on the buttons and drop-down menus I'd like to include on mine, studied color combinations, fonts, and graphics. I looked at black screens, pink backgrounds, and everything in between. Some were simple, yet clean, while others were busy.

After I made a list of what I'd like on my website, I supplied pages and pages of copy—probably twenty-five or more—and told my webmaster what I'd like included on my home page. Every website is unique and should reflect your style, tone, and genre(s).

Here are the pages I chose to include:

Welcome – This is my home page and always features my newest releases with the cover, blurb, and a buy link to Amazon. Do not forget the buy link! If someone is intrigued by your blurb or loves the cover, but there's nowhere to click to purchase it, you may lose a sale. I also include the genres I write along the top right of my home page, as well as my photo, and the covers of my books across the banner.

About – If you click on this button, a drop-down menu appears with three items: Bio, Author Q&A, and 25 Wild & Crazy Things about me. As mentioned, readers like to know the author behind the book.

Novels – The drop-down menu includes each of my novels (listed separately) with a snippet of reader reviews.

Nonfiction – I included my pandemic project, *The Quarantine Cookbook* and this book, *I Wrote a Book. Now What?* When it's released, I'll also add the follow-up: *I'm*

Published. Now What?

Blog – My poor, poor neglected blog rests here. I've had so much news over the past year that I haven't shared in a timely manner. I'm shaking my head. Blogs are great for posting news, awards, announcements, and new releases. However, I sadly often forget my abandoned blog. Shame on me. Don't be like me. Keep your blog updated.

Kids' Books – My children's picture books are listed separately. Each one has a drop-down menu which shows the cover, back-cover blurb, and a link to Amazon and/or Barnes & Noble. I also include fan photos and letters from kids in this section.

Fun Stuff – This page is just what it says—for fun—and features printable coloring pages, bookmarks, and some of my favorite quotes. I also added information about my private reader group, Beth's Book Babes, with a contact form for interested readers.

More Writing – There are two sections: Six-Word Memoirs, as well as several anthologies that have published my short stories or poems. I had forgotten that I included this section until I researched my website for this book. What an enjoyable trip down memory lane.

News – The drop-down menu includes my official bio, social media links, awards, headshots, and news stories.

Contact – It's very important to have a contact page where readers, publishing professionals, and reporters can reach out to you. In the past two weeks, I received two requests from different people who want me to write their life story. The one that caught my attention is a representative for a Hollywood actress. He left his phone number but didn't mention her name. I'm intrigued, to say the least but doubt that I'll delve into this project since I'm sorely behind on my own books. But, see, if I didn't have a way for strangers to contact me, this never would have happened. What should I do? Kidding. Sort of. I think I'll at least return the call and find out the name of this famous actress. It would be rude, otherwise, plus I must know.

As you can see, websites take a lot of work and thought. But they're a necessity. Please add this chore to your must-do list. After I secured the webmaster/designer, I gave her my ideas, emailed my book covers, blurbs, buy links, and while she created the design and showed me various color combinations, I wrote the rest of the copy. Remember that industry professionals may be reading your website. Make it as inviting, unique, and newsworthy as possible.

I'd say my webmaster, Jan, and I spent two months on my website design, off and on. Your website can be as complicated or as simple as you want. If you aren't familiar with an author website, take a look at mine and Google your favorite author sites. It'll give you a great idea of the look you want to achieve and which pages you want to highlight. Remember to update your site with each new release.

On a personal note, I don't care for black backgrounds. I think they're hard to read, but if you write paranormal or thrillers, I can see why authors go this route. Also, please use readable fonts and make sure they aren't miniscule. Consider readers who are of a certain age and may not have the best eyesight. Baby Boomers, like me, are getting older, you know.

PITCHING TO AGENTS & EDITORS

"It's hard to beat a person who never gives up." ~Babe Ruth

PITCHING TO AGENTS & EDITORS

In my opinion, pitching is the scariest part of publishing, but it needn't be. Writers are often introverted and make themselves sick at the thought of pitching their book to an industry insider. Always remember, everyone puts their pants on the same way. I wish I had realized that years ago. You'll see what I mean after you read about my pitching woes.

Also, and this isn't to lower your writerly expectations, but don't get dismayed when you receive rejections. You will. It's part of the process. We've all gotten them. Some famous authors have gotten more than a hundred. A few wallpaper their walls with them, frame the rejections, or stick them in a file for review—and maybe some gloating—after they're eventually published. And, sad but true, some agents and editors never respond to queries.

About ten years ago, I pitched to one agent I followed daily who shall go unnamed. This literary agent posted all kinds of helpful tips and seemed extremely approachable. Once I polished my query letter, I sent it off. I just knew we would have incredible chemistry as an agent and author and was confident she'd like my work.

She never responded.

I checked my email each morning for months and was crushed to say the least. I also stopped following her. Maybe that's childish, but there are plenty more eager agents.

Beginning writers are sensitive. Our feelings are on our sleeves, and it doesn't take much to crush our dreams. It took me a few weeks before I queried again. But I did. I picked myself up and forced myself to attend several local, regional, and national conferences where I pitched *in person* to agent and editors. I remember flying to a state I had never been and where I didn't know a soul except a couple of writers I had met online. This was before Uber, and I trusted a total stranger to pick me up from the airport. She turned out to be an avid reader and we're still friends on Facebook. I took her to dinner as a thank you.

At the four-day conference, I devoured every workshop on craft, studied my pitching notes in my hotel room, and went to the bar at the end of the day—because most writers do this to network. It's a fun, relaxed way to connect while our brains are imploding from all of the newfound information.

As I sipped chardonnay and attempted conversation with strangers who were also nervous, I took comfort in the fact that we're all the same. Many of these aspiring writers were from different states and countries. I met authors from New Zealand, Canada, and China. That alone was worth the price of admission. After I finished my wine, I retreated to my hotel room since my pitch was the following day. I wanted to study the notes I had packed in my suitcase and practice privately in front of the hotel mirror. It may sound silly, but when you're given just ten minutes to introduce yourself, pitch your novel and come up with an elevator pitch—just like the taglines we'll discuss soon—it's daunting. I wanted to familiarize myself with what I wanted to convey—not memorize it—but be comfortable with what I would say, plus I needed to time myself to make sure I could stay within the ten-minute timeframe

That morning, I attended a few more workshops before retreating to my hotel room with a cup of coffee. I wanted to be alert when pitching to a well-known agent from New York

City. I checked the clock, got on the bed with my notes, and reread them aloud twice. As I glanced over my notes, I felt a strange sensation on my face. I peered in the mirror and I saw hives. *Hives.* I had worked myself into such a frenzy that my body was crying out. At least the hives were my skin color. I endeavored to calm myself by breathing in and out, Zen-like, though I felt the opposite of calm and half wondered if I needed a doctor. Maybe I was having an allergic reaction. I decided it was nerves and flung my notes on the bed, checked the mirror again, and attempted to cover my hives with powder. I made my way to the elevator in search of the conference room where this scary agent was holding court.

As the elevator pinged, I stepped down the hallway with fake confidence. I breathed in and out, trying to get rid of my stupid hives. When I arrived a few minutes before my appointed time, I saw a line of other authors and noticed a woman keeping time at the conference room door. She told me another author was inside. I bobbed my head, mouth dry, and noticed my folded notes were damp from sweat. I managed to smile and act as though I were seeing an old friend. When it was my time to go inside, a beautiful, young female agent introduced herself and shook my sweaty hand. Before I had barely sat down, I rattled off several of my publishing credits that didn't have a thing to do with my novel. She was excited to hear about the six-word memoirs. I even had the book with me where my memoir was on page one. When I realized I had been talking far too long about that book and not about my novel, I got to my punchline as the timekeeper poked her head inside the door and said, "Two minutes."

Oh, my God. I had blabbered eight of the allotted ten minutes, which only allowed the agent to ask me questions for two minutes. What a disaster. I expected my hives to cover my entire body at that point. Unbelievably, she requested a partial —the first three chapters—but eventually passed on my novel. I was devastated.

Lesson learned: Talk about your own darn book!

I noticed another agent down the hall, and somehow managed to garner a timeslot. She, too, was kind and gentle, and within a couple of months, ended up sending me a long, handwritten note of rejection. She basically said she really enjoyed my novel but already represented authors in my women's fiction genre. I still have her note.

Once, I pitched to a somewhat scary agent who had extremely long, pointy nails that totally distracted me. She was also an author but as intimidating as hell. I'm not sure why. I actually like long nails, but she didn't smile. Not once. I didn't break out in hives, but when she asked if I had any questions for her, I said, "No." What a stupid response. I could tell by the look on her face that she thought it was stupid too. Of course, I had questions, such as, "How do you find time to promote authors when you have your own books to write and tout?" But did I ask that? No. I was too frightened.

Sometimes I don't think agents and editors realize the power they hold over authors. Maybe they do, but some probably get numb to how we feel when we first begin this journey.

I always enjoy hearing about other authors' journeys. It's helpful to me, and I hope my pitch stories are helpful to you. Hopefully, my crazy experiences will make rejection easier for you in the future. I wish I had read about authors' pitching stories before I jumped in with both feet. It would have softened the blow, and maybe I wouldn't have broken out in hives. Maybe this is spiteful, which I don't mean to be because she was kind and simply doing her job, but I really wish I could tell that agent about what I've accomplished so far, my series, my loyal readers, my more than one thousand reviews in the United States and abroad, and multiple top awards, but I can't remember her name!

HOW I GOT MY TRADITIONAL BOOK DEAL

You will never believe how I became traditionally published. *Never.* But I'll tell you.

Years ago, I came across an online pitching session via the Savvy Authors' site. I believe it was a five-day pitching opportunity involving several publishing houses, editors, and agents. Agents and editors listed several genres they were seeking each day. What? I didn't have to pack, nor get on a plane or book a hotel room? Count me in.

There was only one problem.

The instructions said to boil down our pitch to two sentences. Meaning, tell about your 400-page book in just two sentences. The task seemed impossible.

As I considered my 85,000-word debut, *Thursdays At Coconuts*, I jotted down a few notes. What was it about? Basically, it's about three thirty-something best friends who've reconnected after high school. They each have vastly different careers, boyfriends (or not), and all lead chaotic personal lives. They meet weekly for Happy Hour at Coconuts. For good measure, I threw in several off-the-wall secondary characters, plot twists, humor, cliffhangers, and heartwarming scenes.

Problem is, what I just told you isn't catchy, nor is it the required two sentences. I considered my main characters, the plot, and came up with this pitch, which is also my tagline:

BFFs, sexy bad-boy cops, hippies, and neurotic brides.
What could go wrong?

This pitch immediately tells the reader or publishing authority the type of characters that are in my novel, and showcases obvious humor and conflict that's sure to come. My online pitch netted eight requests from publishers, agents, and editors. Some asked for a partial, which generally means the first three chapters or the first fifty pages. Others asked for a full, which means the entire manuscript.

That was exciting. And, bonus, no hive-inducing moments. Twitter often has online pitch sessions like this. More about hashtags, plus Twitter's #PitMad and #Pitchwars in another section.

By now, you know the importance of boiling your work down, the many ways you can try to attract a publishing professional—whether in person at a conference or online—and about the dreaded rejection. As painful as it was, I wanted the validation from someone other than my mom to tell me my novel was worth publishing. But that's me. Many authors wish to forego this process and take control of their book's destiny themselves. They prefer to self-publish, also called indie publishing, which I'll address next.

Finally, traditional publishing contracts have nuances as far as release dates, and how long your book will be tied up with your publisher, usually five years. Contracts vary from publisher to publisher but likely will cover these items:

✓ Whether you will receive eBooks only or eBook and print options.
✓ How your book will be priced, eBook and paperback.
✓ How many professional edits you'll receive.
✓ How your cover art will be handled.
✓ Release date.
✓ What your author price will be for buying print books from the publisher.
✓ Any marketing the publishing house offers.
✓ Whether you obtain audio rights.
✓ Ditto for film or television rights.

✓ And again for international rights.

Publishing contracts differ, and like my dad likes to say, "Are as dry as a bone." But take time to read the fine print. If you have an agent, they'll be involved too.

I'D RATHER INDIE PUBLISH

After reading about my pitching experiences, you may be shaking your head and thinking you simply want to bypass the whole sweaty hands, hive-inducing process and forego traditional publishing. That's perfectly fine. Many of my author friends have indie published, and several are more successful than me, plus they control their book(s) destiny. There's a lot to say about that, and in fact, I indie published the book you're reading. I also indie published my pandemic cookbook, *The Quarantine Cookbook*, which won a gold medal in the Readers' Favorite International Book Awards. Same for my holiday novella, *Miracle On Aisle Two*, which won a silver medal in 2020, so as I mentioned earlier, I'm a hybrid author. There are advantages to both worlds.

Indie publishing, also called self-publishing, is much more widely accepted than it was a decade ago. Writers have learned that professional covers and well-edited books are a must if you go this route. Those two steps are of utmost importance. Self-publishing used to have a bad name because eager authors didn't take the time to get professional edits or have appealing covers made before clicking the Publish button and sending their books into cyberspace. If a book is riddled with spelling or punctuation errors, or has a bad cover, the book probably won't be widely read, the reviews will be horrible, or both. No one wants that, especially when you're starting out.

Over the years, authors learned this lesson the hard way. Now, it's difficult to tell the difference between an indie book and a traditionally published book. They're all polished, well-written, have beautiful covers, and are as error free as humanly possible. Always remember, your book will be competing for valuable shelf space on Amazon, Barnes & Noble, and other retailers' virtual sites, as well as—hopefully—brick and mortar bookstores. If your cover looks like your first-grade neighbor designed it or if you chose a hideous font that's unreadable when it's a thumbnail size online, you've lost the battle before you even began.

You definitely don't want a nasty one-star review pulling down the average of all of your reviews. It happens, but do everything you can to avoid this type of preventable negative feedback.

So, the question is whether to traditionally publish or indie publish. Or try the third option and be a hybrid author. You should know that for some reason, a few people are still snooty about self-publishing. When I first became a traditionally published author, I remember more than one person put their nose in the air and asked if I had self-published. When I explained I was traditionally published, they made eye contact, smiled, and decided my book was a great accomplishment. This mindset is annoying. Don't let narrow-minded people who do not understand the many options available in publishing bother you. It's your dream, your journey, and your choice.

Of course, if you go the indie route, Amazon will take a percentage of your sales, just like any publisher. The percentage will vary depending on how your book is priced. You can research this through Amazon's KDP program. Traditional publishers include cover art and two or three rounds of professional editing at no cost. Of course, they take also take a percentage of your royalties for this work. And if you have an agent, they get a percentage as well. No matter which route you go, good luck, do your homework, and enjoy the journey.

QUERY LETTER TIPS

If you decide to traditionally publish, you'll need a query letter, which is authorspeak for a cover letter. It's a professional representation of you and the book you're pitching to an agent or editor. Remember, you are up against hundreds, if not thousands, of other aspiring writers, so you want your query to grab the agent's or editor's attention immediately.

Learn how to sell yourself and your work. I know many authors think that is bragging. That drives me crazy, maybe because I worked in marketing and healthcare for years promoting these companies, their products and services, as well as their employees. For the life of me, I do not understand why writers toil away on a manuscript and keep it their little secret. It doesn't make any sense. So, if you're seeking an agent or editor, roll up your sleeves and draft the best query letter you can create. Then, reread it, tweak it, and polish it about fifty times. I'm not kidding. Share it with trusted author friends. Buy someone a cup of coffee or a glass of wine if they're a proofreading pro and great with grammar and punctuation. It's that important.

What's in a query letter, you ask? After I give you the bones of a query letter below, I'll give you several examples in different genres.

First paragraph – This is where you HOOK the agent or editor. Just as you want to hook a reader from the very first line of your work in progress, you must also hook a publishing professional. In the first paragraph, list the book's title, genre, and word count. You might also note any comparisons of your book to, say, television shows or movies. For example, as I've mentioned previously, I bill

Brides At Coconuts as *My Big Fat Greek Wedding* (Italian-style!) meets *Modern Family*. That immediately tells a potential agent or reader that the novel is going to have a big ol' chaotic wedding and a fresh, modern, possibly diverse take, which it does. Note: If you met the agent/editor at a conference or interacted online, definitely mention this to jog their memory.

Second paragraph – Provide the plot—a condensed version of your back-cover blurb—using a few memorable, enticing sentences.

Third paragraph – Include a brief bio, especially if it's relatable to your book. For example if you're a cop or a private investigator and have written a true crime book or a thriller. Also, list any awards, and generally where you're from. The state, region, or country is sufficient. Always end with a polite, "Thank you for taking the time to read my work. I look forward to hearing from you."

Be sure to include your full name and include *all* your contact information—email, phone number, and website. Make it easy for these professionals to contact you.

There are plenty of websites and books on this subject by authors and agents. It's easy enough to Google sample query letters. I also recommend *Writer's Digest*—either their glossy magazine or their online site, for examples of query letters. I had a little fun with sample query letters in a variety of genres. Read on to see what I mean. I can't wait to hear which ones caught your attention.

DEAR AGENT or EDITOR,

First of all, always use their proper name. This is simply how I wanted to title this section.

To recap, query letters are mostly formulaic in that you tell your title, genre, and word count in the first paragraph, describe your plot in the second paragraph, and mention any publishing credentials, awards, and a brief background in the last paragraph. Make doubly sure you have the contact's name spelled correctly, as well as the physical/email address, and whatever you do, don't say, "Dear Sir" or "Dear Madam." For the love of everything publishing, please use their proper names and don't misspell them.

I thought I'd have a little fun with different queries in various genres. I put the sample query letters in italics for easier reading and to set them apart. You will not want to do that. Use a universal, easy-to-read font. Here goes:

Dear Agent Extraordinaire:
I wrote a sci-fi thriller. The word count is 75,000, and my mom really likes it.

This is a joke, of course. Never, ever say this. How about this version instead:

Dear Agent (include proper name):
It was 2099 when aliens ruled the earth—except for one human who had managed to hide in a cave for decades. My sci-fi thriller, ALIENS VERSUS HUMANS is 85,000 words. I'm eager to tell you more.
[Insert more about the plot and your background.]

Heck, I rarely read sci-fi but I'd read this. Would you? Here's another example:

Dear Editor of My Dreams *(use their name, remember):*
I grew up reading the Little House on the Prairie series and yearn for simpler times. After having four children and living on several acres where we homestead, raise cattle and chickens, skip rocks in the creek, and fish, I penned several old-time children's picture books. My newest, SNOW SHOES, is similar to Laura Ingalls Wilder's classic The Long Winter. My kidlit is written in verse at 900 words.
[insert a mini plot and author's bio]

Dear Agent:
My memoir, BASEMENT TO BROADWAY, details my rise to fame after being abused and kept hidden in a basement for nearly a decade. This true story was barely covered by the media because a famous politician was involved. My shocking tale is 65,000 words.
[Add more of the plot, and close with the author's credentials and contact information.]

I probably couldn't resist requesting and reading this. Could you?

Dear Editor*:*
My self-help book will change people's lives. Patent pending, my widget is an everyday gadget. I honestly cannot believe it has never been invented! The word count for YOU NEED THIS is 50,000.

Again, I'd want to read this one too.
See how a compelling opening makes the agent, editor—and reader—want to know more? In fact, they *have* to know more. That's the goal with query letters. Notice the book titles are in all caps. I was taught that's the proper way to type them

in a query letter or synopsis, however, I've noticed a few in italics. Always check submission guidelines to see if the agent or editor has a preference.

By the way, I'm the type of person who will put lip cream meant for vertical lip lines on horizontal lines just to be a rebel. Don't be a rebel with queries. Adhere to the rules and hook that agent/editor/reader!

Disclaimer: I did not research my made-up titles, nor are any of these sample letters real. This is all a figment of my crazy imagination to aid you in your query-letter writing process. By all means, be creative with your letters, and good luck.

PERFECT YOUR BLURB

The dreaded back-cover blurb is almost as frightening as writing a synopsis. Most writers hate doing it, but it's essential to have a short, concise blurb. By the way and just to confuse you further, when you see a short, glowing quotation from one or more authors on another author's cover, that's also called a blurb. I prefer to call them testimonials to avoid misunderstanding. We'll stick with the term blurb for the back cover of your book since that's the proper name.

First, I promise you'll be sick of your blurb by the time you fine tune it fifty times. You'll want concise sentences, powerful words, and three or four short paragraphs. You may get sick of hearing me say to hook the reader in the first couple of sentences, but it's *that* important. We've all learned with social media that people scroll quickly. If you don't grab the agent/editor/publisher/reader's attention quickly, they might not read the entire blurb that you've worked on *forever*. Gasp!

After you draft your blurb go back and cut unnecessary words. Scour it for repeat words, called echoes. In just a few short paragraphs, you definitely do not want to repeat the same adjective or noun. Check everything you wrote carefully, and find the most concise, powerful synonyms you can to describe your novel, kidlit, cookbook, or nonfiction book.

If you're stuck, read blurbs from best-selling authors, whether online or at your favorite bookseller. Notice how succinct they are. See if the hook pulls you in. Is there obvious conflict? Are the characters varied? Is the how-to book something that would be helpful? Is the poignant memoir something you must read? Do the cookbook recipes sound easy and delicious? Are the ingredients easily found? Does the children's book have wonderful illustrations and a sweet or adventuresome story your kids or grands would enjoy?

With millions of books vying for attention, you must write a blurb that entices the reader to carry it to the cash register—or add it to their cart—rather than place it back on the proverbial shelf.

Determine how much information other authors provide and pay attention to what they do or don't give away. With novels, we all know the characters are basically going to go through hell before they have a happy ending. You might mention a few minor spoilers but never give major spoilers away.

When writing a blurb, don't waste valuable space describing a character's hair or eye color or career history. This is premium real estate. For example, I'll say: Wedding planner Suzy, or bank marketer Alex, high school counselor Hope, or New York socialite Cheri. That's enough of a description and immediately tells their profession. The reader wants an intriguing plot, interesting characters, to know there will be conflict, and a developmental arc to the story—a satisfying beginning, middle, and end.

Blurbs are no easy task, but think of them as a challenge. You can do this. For my *Coconuts* series, my blurbs are four to five paragraphs long because I have one short paragraph for each of my four main characters. You can read all of my blurbs (for my novels, cookbook, and children's books) on my author page on Amazon or my website www.bethcarter.com.

Have fun with this task and draft three or four possibilities. Ask fellow authors or readers for input before you finalize this important process.

THE DREADED SYNOPSIS

Receiving a request for a synopsis may drive some writers to drink. They are daunting to write for some reason, and every author I know hates them. Honestly, they aren't that bad. They're not a carnival ride but they're also not as bad as a spider bite.

What are they? A synopsis encapsulates your entire novel in two or three typewritten pages and tells every single major plot point, even the ending. Yes, you heard that right. You give away the ending and any key plot twists along the way. Writers are aghast by this. At least I was. Novelists work hard to drop red herrings while writing to surprise the reader. Telling what happens is counterintuitive to us, but it's what agents and publishers expect before they decide whether our work is worth their effort to edit and publish.

That concept was extremely hard for me. I couldn't believe anyone wanted to know the ending before they even read the novel. Talk about a spoiler alert. But editors and agents are busy people. They can tell by your plot, characters, conflict, and resolution whether your story ends satisfyingly and if they want to commit the time to read your entire manuscript.

Another reason writers don't like creating a synopsis—besides having to boil down 350 pages to two or three pages—is there's no room for flowery prose or those lovely descriptions we agonize over. Basically, you just include the facts with little room for creativity. I still think it's possible for your voice to shine through.

When creating a synopsis, include:

✓ Your name and address in the top left.

- ✓ Genre and word count top right.
- ✓ Place your title in the middle.
- ✓ Either double space or use 1.5 spacing for readability. Use a familiar, professional font. Nothing fancy. Also, indent each new paragraph by five spaces.
- ✓ Beginning with the first paragraph in your novel, go in the exact order your story unfolds. I find it easiest to have a pen and paper beside my laptop, start with Chapter One, and make note of major plot points in each chapter, in order. Leave off minor secondary characters or plot points.
- ✓ When introducing each new character, put their full name in all caps. After they're introduced, first names are sufficient, and at this point, use regular capitalization. This immediately shows how many main characters you have and makes them easily identifiable.
- ✓ Show conflicts and quickly tell how issues are resolved.
- ✓ Describe the ending, which is incredibly hard. I weep every time. Not really. I rarely cry, but you get the gist.
- ✓ I was going to show a synopsis from one of my novels as an example, but I'd rather you read the book to learn organically how it ends. See why that rule is so hard on authors?

Research examples of a synopsis. You'll be able to find many. When you're beginning this writing journey, Google—and craft books—will be your best friend. I constantly explored publishing criterion like this because, like you, I didn't know where to begin. By the way, if you're writing a nonfiction book, you will submit a query letter and a book proposal rather than a synopsis. You can easily find examples of book proposals online as well.

Remember to always be professional and gracious when

querying. Agents and publishers are busy—and they're friends with one another. I've read horror stories where agents said an author lashed out because they rejected them. Some have even done this online for all to see. Ack. Publishing professionals talk among themselves. Don't ruin your chances before you get started.

FINDING AGENTS & PUBLISHERS

If you're seeking a literary agent, a great resource is QueryTracker.net. This site has made the *Writer's Digest* favorite websites list for years, which gives me great confidence. It's also kept current.

QueryTracker has a database of nearly two thousand agents who are actively seeking a variety of fiction and nonfiction submissions. There's a link to each agent's website. Take the time to study each agent's submission guidelines, and see if your genre is a fit before querying. If the agent is closed to submissions or does not represent your genre, do not query them. Simply move on to another agent. You'll find many to choose from.

Additionally, many agents have blogs with helpful querying tips. Read them to get a feel for the books and authors they represent. Before I was published, I stalked the blog of Janet Reid, a well-known literary agent a.k.a. the Query Shark. She enjoys—maybe a little too much—ripping beginning writers' queries to shreds. Publicly. But the authors agree to this before sending her queries, so they know what they're getting into. I also follow Janet Reid on Twitter. I even found a mistake on a pinned post and hesitantly, reluctantly, told her via private message. She thanked me! Whew. Close shark encounter. Janet Reid's blog often showcases good and bad query letters, as well as other valuable publishing advice. Remember, this agent is not afraid to use her red pen and make the sender's query letter bleed. I stalked, I mean followed, her religiously when I first started out. I gleaned a great deal of information about what you should and should not include when contacting an industry professional. If you're brave, wade into the water.

Another way to glean information about dream agents and publishers is to search Publisher's Marketplace and scan the recent publishing deals. If you plan to query a certain agent or publishing house, see what type of book they've had success selling. Then, query that agent, or a junior agent with the same agency. Likely, they'll share the same contacts and you just might be the next one listed on that fabulous site. Always do your homework when seeking representation. Best of luck if you go this route.

PITMAD: AN EXCITING OPTION FOR FINDING AGENTS

Another unique, quick way to attract the attention of literary agents and publishers is something called PitMad. Using the hashtag, #pitmad, you'll discover a pitch party on Twitter on certain dates. PitMad was founded by *New York Times* bestselling author Brenda Drake. She also started #pitchwars and has a website with detailed information. Be sure you have a clean manuscript and a query letter ready to go, or nearly ready, in case an agent reaches out and wants to read more, which is always the goal.

Here's how it works:

- ✓ Find the date for a #pitmad event on Twitter by following the hashtag.
- ✓ Study past #pitmad tweets to see which ones made you want to read a particular novel. Never copy, but rather, see what works and what doesn't. You'll find many intriguing pitches, and this will also help you know what to post in the future.
- ✓ Create a pitch using 280 characters or less.
- ✓ Use the hashtag #pitmad as well as hashtags to identify your genre. For instance, I'd use #WF for women's fiction and #PB for children's picture books or #cookbook or #romcom or #dramedy. Those all fit with my novels and kidlit. For this book, I'd use #authorship #marketing #aspiringauthors and #nonfiction, for example.

Whether you write #scifi #MG for middle grade #horror #mystery #memoir or whatever the genre, PitMad is generally open to a wide variety of genres.

✓ Only industry professionals—agents and publishers—should Favorite PitMad tweets, so writers should avoid doing this.

✓ However, share away. This means retweet. And if other writers retweet your pitch, by all means, return the favor.

✓ Another tip is to use comparable titles to describe your book. For example, a comp I've mentioned previously is: *My Big Fat Greek Wedding* (Italian-Style!) meets *Modern Family*. I use this comparison to promote *Babies at Coconuts*, because it starts out with a wedding about a crazy Italian family that clashes with an American family while the two grooms wed. There's also a baby, obviously, as per the title. By using comps, this immediately gives the agent a feel for your novel. Only use movies or television shows that are familiar to the masses. An obscure, foreign film with subtitles would not work in your favor.

✓ Be sure to pin your #pitmad pitch tweet to the top of your page on the scheduled day so it doesn't get buried among your other retweets about funny memes and dog or cat photos.

✓ Ask your followers to #RT to get more eyes on your pitch.

WORKING WITH A CHILDREN'S BOOK PUBLISHER

If you're interested in writing children's books, this chapter is for you. If you're not, feel free to skip to the next section, although the information is useful for all genres, and you'll likely relate to my enthusiasm and ensuing anguish.

As I said in the intro, I switched gears from novel writing to children's books to find joy after our shocking family tragedy. Over the years, I've discovered kidlit is a delightful, creative, highly rewarding outlet.

When I penned my first children's picture book, *What Do You Want to Be?* I wasn't published by the first publisher I sent my manuscript to. The publisher held onto it for nine long months with zero response. I waited and waited and finally grew impatient about being ignored. This was early in my career when I didn't always make the best choices.

After I sent a couple of emails, she finally responded with, "You'll hear from me this weekend" or "You'll see the illustrations next week." It was radio silence for several more weeks. She wanted her son to do the illustrations, so I asked for samples of his work. Again, nothing. Fed up, I finally sent an email to terminate our verbal agreement and started my search all over again. Be patient for as long as you can, but don't be afraid to walk away.

I found another children's publisher via Facebook. I had befriended another kidlit author and noticed the publisher's name on her Facebook page. For grins, I Googled the site and looked at the author bios, as well as the illustrated book covers. I liked them. On the website, the authors each had their own page, including their photo, bio, the book cover, and a blurb about their book.

I decided to choose three authors at random from the website to ask questions about their experience. I emailed them and asked if they liked the publisher, were happy with the quality of their books, the illustrations, and if they would use the publisher again. All said "yes." My unscientific sampling was good enough for me. It's important to do your due diligence.

I promptly emailed my manuscript to the editor, and he responded quickly—in two weeks. He said he liked my story, the rhyme, and said it was the perfect length. I wondered if that meant he wanted to publish it. I wasn't sure. I hoped so but was so excited by his quick response that I was almost afraid to jinx it by asking such an obvious question.

Still wondering, we drove to Texas for the birth of our first granddaughter. After six hours of driving, we pulled into the parking lot of a restaurant and my phone rang. It was the editor. I mouthed to my husband, "It's him." He nodded, understanding. Lord knows I had talked enough about wanting to get published that he knew I had to take the call. After a forty-minute conversation, the publisher assured me he, indeed, wanted to publish my manuscript. He requested my bio, headshot, and hung up, promising to send sample illustrations and an agreement. As I sat in the restaurant, elated, I could barely eat. I was on my way.

For a month, I worked with the editor on the layout and edits for my first picture book. Then, I spent another month or two working with the illustrator. We added a few items and changed the direction of a character's ballet arm three times—it started out looking like John Travolta's famous pose from *Saturday Night Fever*. I'm dating myself but you've surely seen this iconic movie. The artist changed the ballet pose to yet another variation but the character's arm looked broken. Frustrated, the editor emailed and said he was tired of working on this illustration. He told me I was becoming one of his most bothersome authors. Staring at his response on the screen, I couldn't breathe and nearly cried. I thought he'd never work with me again. I explained I was scattered, excited, and highly traumatized after our family tragedy.

You see, I was working on a eulogy for my niece's husband, plus an impact statement for my beloved niece's murder trial. Seeing joyful illustrations were my happy place but, at the same time, I felt schizophrenic. I had extreme highs and extreme lows, like the rest of the family, especially my sister, her other daughter, and our mother. Nothing was as it should be. It still isn't in some regards. I wanted to crawl into bed and stay there for months. After I explained the heartbreak, the editor took everything into consideration and decided I wasn't so bothersome after all. Since then, he has published three more of my children's books and they've gone smoothly.

Hopefully, your journey will be much easier. If you decide to write a children's book, pay close attention to the illustrator's art and make sure it's a good representation of your words. Of course, illustrators need to have leeway to be creative but I discovered errors are easily made. I had one character scratching his left knee but the illustrator had him scratching his right knee. I wrote that the teacher, Mrs. McGee, was standing by her desk but the artist drew her sitting at her desk. It's important to pay attention to every detail. Kids, parents, and teachers will notice.

I've loved the journey of writing children's books and have drafted several more. I received my first fan letter from a six-year-old named Grace. Her mom posted it on my Facebook page years ago. On the envelope, Grace addressed it to: "The Princess of Writing." I was overcome. It doesn't get any better than that. I'll always cherish her letter. I've gone to several schools where the kids sat riveted listening to me read my book and hearing about the writing process. I encouraged them to write stories of their own, took a small stuffed pig, and had them name the character. I told the young students all stories need conflict and asked them what could be a problem for a pig. There were several lively answers and we settled on having him get stung by a bee.

When I read my first and most popular picture book, *What Do You Want to Be?,* I always tell students to dream big and ask them what they'd like to be when they grow up. The kids raise their hands—or shout out—a variety of specific occupations from jewelry maker to heart surgeon. Some want to be a mommy or teacher while others want to be an astronaut or in the Army. My favorite answer was from a kindergartner: "I want to be a canoe."

Once, I received a packet of tiny, folded handwritten paper books from a class of first graders after I spoke to them at school in a small, rural town. The students drew their own illustrations on the cover along with a sweet story inside. Many students drew a portrait of me, which was funny and touching. Those letters are in my office and are treasured keepsakes. From that point, I was hooked on writing for kids.

WRITING CONFERENCES & CONTESTS

Pitching also occurs at writer conferences. Often, writers' groups have annual events where agents and publishers are present, as do annual national conventions. The bigger conventions offer a quick pitching format, akin to speed dating. Several agents and editors participate in these.

There are book conventions for every genre imaginable—some are even held on cruise ships. Investigate writers' conferences in your genre or area, make a list, and decide how many you want to attend each year. I normally attend two or three.

If agents or publishers request your work, this is a fabulous way to be seen and possibly get your foot in the door.

In addition to in-person pitches, I know several writers who submitted their first three paragraphs to literary contests that were judged by industry professionals. Many made connections this way, through the mail, and what could be easier? Okay, you have to polish your manuscript and research the agents, but after you do your homework, hit Send.

What do you have to lose? Tweak your first three chapters until they shine like a car off the factory line. Then, submit, submit, submit. There's generally a list of contests in the back of writerly magazines, or simply Google contests for your genre.

That said, I have a *but*. There's always a but, isn't there. Don't get so hung up on winning contests that it's all you do.

I know authors who do this. Every year, they submit to several contests hoping to attend a banquet and win a certificate, ribbon, or trophy. It's really fun. I've done it. We long for validation and adulation from fellow authors, plus getting to dress up after working in pajamas or yoga pants all year is a bonus. But you have to move beyond contests at some point, finish your manuscript, and start the next book.

GRAMMAR
& PUNCTUATION

GRAMMAR & PUNCTUATION TIPS

I can almost hear some of you groaning. Don't yawn or flip the page. Please. Grammar and punctuation rules are important, especially before you query an agent or editor. You want your query and manuscript to be as pristine as humanly possible. I happen to love both topics but realize many writers don't feel the same. However, it's part of our profession—an important, essential part of our craft.

Sure, writers can hire editors, and should, but if you indie publish and turn in a hornet's nest of a manuscript, don't you think a writer with a clean manuscript will float to the top of an agent's slush pile? Of course, it would, so let's embrace this sometimes pointy subject. Enjoy wine or a cocktail of your choice later to celebrate learning the tips in this section. It won't hurt. I promise.

Once I held a seminar on this topic at the private college where I worked. I gave the staff plenty of oral and written examples on communication, grammar, and punctuation. I'll never forget the college security guard, Jim, who was a friend and former classmate. He came up to me afterward and said, "My boss told me to take this class. I thought it would be boring, but you made it interesting and fun." I was thrilled. That's the goal.

I guess I'm a nerd, but I love these topics. I'm going to touch on a few helpful punctuation and grammar tips that writers often use incorrectly, even bestselling authors. Don't worry. I won't go overboard. After all, this isn't a grammar book. Let's start with some obscure terms I learned in college.

The Subjunctive Mood – Doesn't that sound sexy? Well, only to punctuation nerds. The subjunctive mood doesn't have anything to do with candles, bubble baths, or crooners, sadly, but it will make your writing stand out. Here's an example:

I wish I *were* a best-selling author.

If I *were* rich, I would quit my job.

Notice that even though the subject is singular, you use "were" instead of "was." I see writers make this mistake quite often. Two big clues to know whether you're in the subjunctive mood are the words "if" and "wish." Easy, right? Don't you feel smarter already?

The Oxford Comma – Writers and English professors love the Oxford comma debate. We're a tad weird that way. An Oxford comma is used by placing a comma before the word "and" in a series. In a nutshell, that's it. Simple, right? Here's an example:

Oxford comma: Bob hung a red, white, and blue flag.

If you take out the Oxford comma, and say:

Bob hung a red, white and blue flag. This could mean Bob hung one red flag and possibly a blue and white Scottish flag. By using the Oxford comma, it clearly spells out the three colors of one flag.

Periods Inside Quotation Marks

When using dialogue—or in a letter, for that matter—always place punctuation marks inside quotation marks. Here's an example:

"Are you enjoying this book?" Beth asked.

"Tell me your favorite section," Beth said.

By the way, see how I wrote *Beth asked* and *Beth said* at the end of the sentence? When I wrote my first novel, I was accustomed to feature writing, essays, and news articles I'd written where you do this in reverse, i.e., *said Beth* or *asked Beth*. When my editor told me I had to change all of those dialogue tags on more than four hundred pages, I filled up a wineglass or two. What a nightmare, especially since I didn't realize I could have done that with the Find/Replace keys. Sigh. I hope this helps you avoid that woeful, time suck of a trap.

When to Hyphenate Words – When two words modify a noun, i.e., short-term position or well-written book, you use a hyphen to basically "hook" the words together. We all know what short term means—a position that's temporary—so why is the hyphen necessary? To test this rule, take one of the words out. If one word won't stand on its own, for example, neither short position, nor term position make sense. Therefore, a hyphen is necessary since both words, short and term, modify the noun. Likewise, in the case of a well-written book, the same rule applies. A well book doesn't make sense (unless it's a book about wells) nor does a written book in this context.

Here are more easy-to-understand examples:

Tom enjoyed skiing down snow-covered mountains.

Anna's fur-like coat drew angry glances.

George's mind-boggling novel kept Grace up at night.

Exception: Isn't there always a darn exception to every rule? You knew there had to be one, right? When one of the words modifying a noun ends in "ly," you drop the hyphen. Example: "I love the smell of freshly baked bread."

I can hear you groaning. Now, I know how English teachers felt. No hyphen is needed since freshly ends in "ly." Boom. Got it?

The Problem Children: Me, Myself, & I

The misuse of me, myself, and I drives me a tad bonkers. It's one of my many pet peeves. Please learn how to use these terms properly. You'll make your readers and editors happy.

Surprisingly, I notice authors use these words incorrectly often. And it isn't just writers. I worked at a private university in the president's office for seven years. Once, the dean of the business college called to ask whether he should use "I" or "me" in a sentence. He had a doctorate and I was an executive secretary, a single mom at the time, while attending college at night. Thoroughly impressed that he was not ashamed to ask for assistance, I asked the dean to give me an example of his sentence so I could hear it in context. It was about tennis.

The late Dr. Strube and his wife simply wanted to know if another couple would join them for a tennis match. I told him the correct grammar could go both ways, depending on whether "I" or "me" was at the beginning or at the end of the sentence. The conversation went back and forth as I gave him a couple of possibilities.

Correct: Would you and your wife like to join Susan and me for tennis?"

The easiest way to tell which way is correct is to take the other person's name out of the sentence. For example, you wouldn't say, "Would you and your wife like to join I for tennis?" Doesn't this sound silly? Yet, I see people write this often on social media. They'll post pictures of themselves with family members and say, "Here's my husband and I on our anniversary." That's incorrect. You wouldn't say, "Here's I on vacation." The proper phrasing should be: "Here's my husband and me on our anniversary."

Finally, whatever you do, please do not insert "myself" into this equation. I say strike that word from your vocabulary since it's rarely correct. I've seen writers say, "Myself and my husband went on vacation." Would you ever say: "Myself went on vacation." Of course not. It's the same if you use myself at the end of the sentence. That's also incorrect. Write down the word myself, wad it up, and toss it in the trash.

When to Capitalize Pronouns

I often see writers and business people confuse this rule as well.

Correct: I had lunch with my dad.

You don't capitalize Dad because the word "my" is in front of the pronoun.

Also correct: I had lunch with Dad.

Correct: Have you tasted Mom's blackberry cobbler?

Also correct: Blackberry cobbler is my mom's specialty.

There are two easy tips to get this right: If the word "my" comes before a pronoun, that's a telltale way of knowing you shouldn't capitalize the word. Also, try inserting a person's proper name in the place of dad/mom/editor/friend/neighbor. If it doesn't make sense, i.e., "I had lunch with my Beth," do not capitalize it. Easy peasy, right?

Use Commas Around Proper Names – When you're addressing someone in correspondence or in a book, use commas before and after their name, such as:

Beth, just tell me how to get published.

Please stop with the punctuation lessons, Beth, I'm getting a headache.

I'm glad you covered punctuation, Beth.

But, Beth, don't editors handle this?

Okay, Beth, we get it. Let's move on.

One thing that will impress agents and editors is if you follow the *Chicago Manual of Style*, for instance. When you query editors, peruse their website to see if they have a style preference. For instance, mine requires the Oxford comma and also prefers using the singular version of backward and forward, rather than backwards and forwards, which is still accurate. You'll find out soon enough from your editor, but you'll be ahead of the game if you are aware of their stylistic preferences early on.

Use Punctuation When Addressing Someone

Similarly to the examples above, if you or your characters are addressing someone, a comma is necessary. We've probably all seen this hilarious example on social media:

Do your best, man.

Do your best man.

Yikes. See the glaring difference? Punctuation could save a marriage!

In my novel, *Cowboys At Coconuts*, the socialite and her eventual cowboy boyfriend often refer to each other by nicknames. You also put a comma before and after nicknames or pet names, like this:

"Kiss me, Cowboy. I'll explain later."

"Why do you have red paint on the sole of your shoes, New York?"

Use Commas When Greeting Someone

If your characters are greeting someone, always use a comma to set off the greeting, such as:

"Hey, sorry I was late."

Tucker stood to shake the attorney's hand. "Hello, sir. I have a confession."

"Bye, Tucker. Thanks for another great evening."

Who/That/Which

There's only one quick point I want to make about this. People should *always* be referred to as "who" if you're not using their proper name, sex, or profession. Why? Because people are not a thing or a that.

Correct: Alex stared at the flashy newcomer, *who* appeared via limo amid a flurry of camera flashes.

Correct: The woman *who* works at the pharmacy is extremely helpful.

In the majority of written communication I see, whether in a book or online, people nearly always say, "The woman *that* works at the pharmacy is extremely helpful." No! She's a who. Not a that.

So, you might be wondering when to use "that" or "which" and why we have these words to begin with if they're so exasperating. Never fear. They're fine words. Don't get mad at them. That and which are most often used when you're referring to a group, a committee, or a board of directors like this:

The new park board *which* added handicapped accessibility is a Godsend.

Or: The school board *that* approved online learning for two more years is out of its collective mind.

Often, which and that may be interchanged. Enough about that. I couldn't resist.

One Space vs. Two Spaces

For those of us who are, ahem, fifty- or sixty-something, who learned to type on IBM Selectric typewriters with the fancy, silver ball in high school, this section is for you. Our high school teachers drilled into us that two spaces were necessary after every single period, question mark, or exclamation point, remember? I'm sure you do. In fact, I can come close to guessing a person's age if I see an online post where they have two spaces after each sentence.

Guess what? That two-space rule has changed.

In publishing, much to my chagrin when I penned my first novel, my editor told me I had to take out every extra space after every single sentence. Oh, my God. Do you know how many sentences are in a 400-page novel? Too many to count. I'm pretty sure I had cocktails that evening before tackling this daunting chore. I'm not sure whether I could have used the Find/Replace function to accomplish this time-consuming task, but alas, I did it the hard way. Sentence by sentence. Now, my editor says Find/Replace would have done the trick. Oy. That won't happen again.

You can thank me now. I just saved you a week of work. Seriously, I'm not sure why this spacing preference occurred but assume it's due to publishing costs for print books. Whatever the reason, just remember to use only one space after any type of punctuation at the end of a sentence. Hopefully, your typing teacher won't haunt you.

No Commas Before "Too"

Here we go again with changing those pesky rules we all learned in high school and college English classes. Publishers now remove commas before and after the word "too." I *know*. It's maddening because we're so proud of the fact that we remembered this punctuation rule from many years ago. Nevertheless, take it out, and your editor will be happy. It's always something.

Use a Comma to Separate Appositives

This is an easy rule. Simply use a comma to separate descriptive appositives, which are two descriptive elements, before a noun. Often, you can test this by seeing if the word "and" could be inserted between the descriptors. Another way to test this rule is to see if the two words could be used in reverse. It's much cleaner to drop "and" and use a comma instead, such as:

She donned a black, floppy hat.

The diners love my mouthwatering, cheesy meatloaf.

Notice "and" would sound clunky in the first example— She donned a black and floppy hat. It's much cleaner to simply use a comma. Likewise, the words make sense in reverse: She donned a floppy, black hat and/or the diners love my cheesy, mouthwatering meatloaf.

Every comma and word count in a manuscript, especially if you're tightening your prose. Make sure your grammar and punctuation are as close to perfect as you scour your first, second, and third draft. If you need help in this area, hire an editor or buy books on the subject. There are a gazillion more grammar and punctuation rules in the English language, but these are the errors I see most often. I wanted to be a teacher as a kid, so maybe that's my excuse for this section. And...I'm not perfect. Everyone makes grammatical and punctuation blunders. You may find one in this book, but I hope not. It's important to scour your manuscript to get it as close to perfection as possible before querying agents, editors, or clicking "publish" on Amazon. You will come across as a real pro if you learn and embrace these rules. Let's move on.

Beth Carter

MARKETING 101

> "The way to get started is to quit talking and begin doing." ~Walt Disney

BECOME A HASHTAG EXPERT

I assume you're familiar with hashtags, but if you're new to Twitter or Instagram, this may be an unfamiliar term. Writers occasionally mention they are unfamiliar with these platforms. If so, this section is for you.

Hashtags are powerful for connecting with like-minded readers, bloggers, authors, agents, and publishers. A hashtag is what Baby Boomers used to refer to as a pound sign. I'm dating myself. Oh, well. In social media, hashtags are used to identify certain items or people, and groups similar posts with the same tag.

For example, I love quotes by famous people—or anyone, really. Every time I share one, I use the hashtags #quote and #quotes. Go ahead and open your favorite social media platform right now, type #quotes in the search bar, and you'll see what I mean. I'll wait. *drums fingers on the table* Great. You're back. See what I mean? How cool is that.

This is also a fantastic way to connect with other readers using hashtags like:

#readers	#readersofinsta
#readersofig	#amreading
#amreadingromance	#amreadingmystery
#amreadingscifi	#bookblogger
#bookshelf	#booknerd
#booklover	#ilovebooks
#booksofig	#feelgoodbooks

There are too many hashtags to mention here, but you'll catch on quickly. Make friends with fellow readers in your genre, mention you're writing a book, and ask if they'd be interested in giving you feedback. You'll be surprised how reciprocal the writing community is. It's very supportive.

Likewise, if you want to connect with fellow authors, here's a sampling of writerly hashtags:

#debut	#newauthor
#author	#authorslife
#writerslife	#amediting
#amwriting	#amquerying
#writersunite	#writergram
#writersblock	

As you can see, the hashtag opportunities are endless.

One very important hashtag for new authors who are on Twitter is #writerslift. This is where you ask fellow writers and authors to follow you on Twitter, maybe pose a writerly question or ask them to tell about their WIP. I've seen new authors get hundreds of followers in a short span of time by doing this. I actually need to do it more often. It's very effective. The unwritten rule is to follow everyone back.

Tailor hashtags for every book you write, such as:

#mystery	#romance
#scifi	#nonfiction
#kidlit	#cookbook

#selfhelp	#thriller
#paranormal	#memoir
#chicklit	#suspense
#parenting	#blogging
#travel	

Use the appropriate hashtag for whatever genre you're penning. I bet you're nodding along and this hashtag phenomenon is crystalizing about now. Regrettably, punctuation is not used in hashtags, which makes most writers wince. It's hard to keep from using an apostrophe when it's proper.

With every book you write, no matter the genre, these hashtags apply:

#books	#novels
#newrelease	#booklover
#booknerd	#Amazon
#BN (Barnes & Noble)	#ilovebooks
#KU (Kindle Unlimited)	

If you're a professional who is writing a #nonfiction book about your specialty, use the appropriate hashtag to tailor your own genre, such as:

#medicine	#doctor
#engineer	#architecture
#dentist	#teeth
#attorney	#legal
#professor	#college
#military	#WWI
#WWII	#KoreanWar
#CivilWar	#Vietnam
#militarybook	#militaryromance
#psychology	#selfhelp

See, hashtags are easy and will help your audience find

you by using keywords from your novel or book.

There is an outstanding, supportive writing community on Twitter, and I suggest you tag them with questions, shares and RTs (retweets.) I'm sure you can guess that hashtag. Yep. It's #writingcommunity. One day, I noticed it was misspelled three different ways, tweeted about it, and someone cleaned up most of the typos. Horrors. And for a writing community, no less. Sheesh.

When you have a title for your book, you will want to make a hashtag with the name. I'll use my books to show you how I tailor my hashtags. This isn't just to plug them—though, since you're here—just kidding. Sort of.

For my multi-award-winning *Coconuts* series, I use:

#Coconuts	#womensfiction
#romcom	#awardwinningseries
#chicklit	#romance
#romancebook	#romancenovel
#dramedy	#mustread
#ThursdaysAtCoconuts	
#ChaosAtCoconuts	
#BabiesAtCoconuts	
#CowboysAtCoconuts	
#BridesAtCoconuts	

There will be one final book in my series. I haven't yet revealed the title and am supposed to be working on it right now. Oops. If space allows, I might also give potential readers a flavor of my books by using these hashtags:

#heartwarming	#humorous
#funny	#hilarious
#girlfriends	#HappyHour
#BFFs	#cops
#hippies	#brides
#cowboys	#socialite

This tells the reader immediately the type of characters who are in my *Coconuts* novels. Coconuts is their Happy Hour oasis, by the way. I don't use all of these on any one tweet, because there simply wouldn't be enough character space allotted. Mix and match as you please.

For my standalone novel, *Sleeping With Elvis*, I use the following hashtags:

#Elvis	#ElvisPresley
#tributeartists	#entertainers
#KeyLimeIsland	#romance
#suspense	#shipwreck
#drama	#beachread

See how easy this is? Just think about the contents of your novel or nonfiction book and use words that describe the plot and characters.

In my holiday novella, *Miracle On Aisle Two*, I used #pink because the little five-year-old character, Betsy, requested a pink bicycle for Christmas. Surprisingly, I had a lot of people notice that hashtag on Instagram. I also use:

#holiday	#holidayromance
#Christmas	#Christmasbook
#miracle	#sweet
#heartwarming	#feelgood
#allthefeels	#singlemom
#novella	#romance
#sweet	#mustread
#cozy	

I've written four children's picture books: *What Do You Want To Be?*, *The Missing Key*, *Santa's Secret*, and *Sour Power*. For these, I use entirely different hashtags than my novels, including:

#PB (picture book)	#kidlit
#kids	#parents
#teachers	#counselors
#elementaryschool	#librarian
#librarians	#childrensbook

If you write middle ground or young adult, use #MG or #YA.

During the pandemic, I wrote a cookbook aptly titled *The Quarantine Cookbook*. The title is shown on a mask on the front. What a crazy year. As I've mentioned, besides nearly 200 family favorite recipes, I included stay-at-home activities, hilarious food quotes, and six-word memoirs about quarantine life. Additionally, I donated the proceeds during 2020 to Tunnel to Towers. I used these hashtags to promote my cookbook:

#cookbook	#cookbooks
#cookbookauthor	#recipes
#charitycookbook	#Tunnel2Towers
#healthcareheroes	#pandemic
#quarantinecooking	#easyrecipes
#recipes	#deliciousrecipes
#quarantine	#quarantinelife
#COVID	

If you're pitching to agents, you'll want to use #WIP (work in progress) #pitchwars #pitmad #amquerying #ampitching #1linewed (where you tweet a compelling line from your book and hope to catch an agent or editor's eye.) There are many more possibilities. Study the hashtags authors who write in your genre use when pitching their work.

Other helpful hashtags include #writetip and #pubtip. Type those into a search bar on Twitter and you'll find all kinds of helpful info.

As you can see, there's a variety of hashtags for every type of book. It's easy to determine which ones would most benefit your work. Simply consider your genre, setting, characters, plot, title, and most of all, your audience. They're the ones who will type these terms into search engines. You'll want your book to be at the top of their search history.

I'm sure you're a hashtag expert by now. I'll just mention a few more that are important in a writer's life. Many writers are, gasp, morning people. I'm not one of them. But if you are and want to connect with early bird writers, those authors use #5amwritersclub. I, on the other hand, use #afternoonwriter. Other common hashtags for writers include:

#storyteller   #ilovebooks
#ilovereaders   #writerslife
#booklover   #bookclub
#bookclubs   #readers
#readersofinsta   #bookstagram
#books   #novels

You should also include a hashtag for your name, i.e.:

#BethCarter   #author
#AuthorBethCarter   #authorsofig
#romanceauthor   #instaauthor
#authorsofinstagram

As you might imagine, it takes me forever to complete an Instagram post because I add a lot of hashtags, but only a few will suffice as long as you make it easy for potential readers to find you. I think that's enough about hashtags. Someone could probably write an entire book about them—and likely has—but I have many more topics to discuss.

BUILD YOUR PUBLISHING CREDITS

Before you begin querying agents or editors, it's always a good idea to build your publishing credits. Credits could include magazine or newspaper articles, short stories, and poetry, for example.

My credits started small. *Really* small. In fact, aside from my byline in our middle school's newspaper and several articles I wrote when I worked in healthcare and banking, my first fictional publishing credit was just six words:

I got published using six words.

Poignant, right? My daughter had my six-word memoir emblazoned on a tee shirt, which I adore.

Here's another one of my memoirs that was published on page one of *SMITH Magazine's* book*, It All Changed In An Instant*:

Zero. Zip. Zilch. Not published—yet.

I love discussing six-word memoirs because they're unique, concise, and force you to choose powerful words. Six-word memoirs allegedly began when Ernest Hemingway was challenged to write his memoir using this form of micro-flash fiction. Hemingway's sixer was:

For sale: Baby shoes, never worn.

Many stories have been written about this. Hemmingway supposedly won ten dollars—no small sum in the 20s—from fellow writers for his sad tale.

I discovered this micro genre years ago while reading the annual "101 Best Websites" by *Writer's Digest. SMITH Magazine*, home to six-word memoirs, made the list and has for many years. I was intrigued. As I perused the submissions on their website, which ran the gamut—from funny, quirky, inspirational, and sad—I was immediately hooked. I began submitting six-word memoirs nonstop for a few weeks. My OCD kicked in and I couldn't stop.

I soon caught the attention of the editor, Larry Smith, who called me a "power user." He featured one of my memoirs on the front page of his online magazine close to Mother's Day. My MOMoir was: "Moms do it in high heels." I was an online phenomenon. Well, almost.

A few months later, I received a letter from the editor. This time he told me my six-word memoir would be featured in *It All Changed In An Instant,* featuring celebrities, famous authors and little old me. What? I couldn't believe it. The editor informed me they had received more than 200,000 submissions worldwide and around 1,000 were selected for this collection. I was beyond honored and excited. *SMITH* had several promotional book tours. I attended the one in New York City at the 92nd Street Y. Many of the memoirists were featured, and we were invited to read our memoirs aloud. Several impromptu sessions were held with the audience. It was thrilling.

My memoirs have also been published in another collection, *Six Words About Work*, as well as a desk calendar. That's right, I'm a calendar girl. That memoir was:

Midlife Isn't so Bad; Reinvented Myself.

Here are some famous writers published in *It All Changed In An Instant*:

"Former boss: 'Writing's your worst skill!'" ~ Amy Tan
"Life is one big editorial meeting." ~ Gloria Steinem

"Journalism? Hah! Just make stuff up." ~ Dave Barry

Six words can pack a punch and they've been used by teachers in lesson plans, preachers have used them for sermons, as did a reporter who reviewed *SMITH*'s first book using all six-word sentences. National Public Radio is a huge fan and often has the editor on the air with eager callers joining the six-word challenge.

I encourage you to try them. I've sponsored contests where I asked writers to submit six-word memoirs regarding writing life, querying agents, and marketing. They're entertaining and cathartic. See where starting small gets you? I hope you'll try this creative genre. Go to www.sixwordmemoirs.com and get started. I could go on and on about six-word memoirs, but we'll move on. It's great stuff, right?

ANTHOLOGIES

Other ways to build publishing credits include short stories or poems. There are themed anthologies for westerns, romance, mystery, paranormal, sci-fi, or about topical subjects like holidays, social justice, or storm-ravaged towns. I submitted a short story which was accepted for publication in *A Bad Hair Day* Anthology. I couldn't resist that concept.

Simply do some research to see who is seeking submissions. Often a smaller press will combine several authors' stories into one anthology. Publishing credits run the gamut including fiction, nonfiction, fan fiction, short stories, flash fiction, article writing, essays, travel writing, scriptwriting, and blogging, to name a few. Try several different genres to find your sweet spot. You might surprise yourself.

FLASH FICTION

Besides my fondness for six-word memoirs, another great way to tighten your prose is by writing flash fiction. That's often for a 50- to 200-word story. It's also called micro fiction. I used to belong to a group called the Friday Fictioneers on Facebook. I believe it's still active. As the name implies, each Friday after the coordinator posted a photo prompt—usually something obscure—by midweek, the Fictioneers were invited to submit a 100-word flash fiction story. The stories were always entertaining and I was amazed how every writer could stare at the same photo and have an entirely different take. That's the beauty of storytelling.

I participated in the Friday Fictioneers for over a year and am still friends with many writers from this group. It was a great way to add weekly content to my blog, plus using one hundred words forced me to select powerful, visually concise words. I would encourage you to try this. It's a lively, creative group, to boot.

Often, *Writer's Digest* has photo or written prompts listed in their monthly magazine. Go ahead and try it. You might win some cash, as well as bragging rights, and yes, publishing credits.

Another way to tighten your prose is to use the handy Find/Replace button in Word. It's a simple way to see how many times you used words like "very" or "just." Instead of using very, such as: "He talked very loudly," change it to "He bellowed." Much better.

Seek and destroy weak words. You probably already know which words you say too often, and if you don't, an editor will find them. However, your chances for publication will improve if you submit the cleanest manuscript you can.

ESTABLISH AN ONLINE PRESENCE

You'll want to establish a presence on Amazon by going to Author Central and adding your headshot, bio, and the cover of your book(s). Their prompts will walk you through this process, and if you have difficulty, you can contact Amazon via phone or email.

A *real* headshot—not a fish or a flower—is preferable because readers like to see what authors look like. By the way, a current photo is desirable. I believe mine is three years old, and my favorite photo in the red shirt is five years old. I'll get new headshots in a year or two before the wrinkles take over.

I once saw an author's photo, and for years, I thought she was in her late forties. When I saw her at a conference, she was an eighty-year-old woman with white hair. It was a shock. On the one hand, it's quite inspirational that she's active and writing. On the other, readers would walk right past her table looking for her forty-something photo. You definitely want readers to recognize you when you're in person at a book signing or conference.

For each site, you'll also want to add a succinct, catchy bio describing the genre you write, where you're from, any awards you've received, and/or a catchy phrase that lets readers know a little about what you're like in your private life. For instance, I've already mentioned I love to shop at T.J. Maxx. I also tell readers I write while sipping a skinny vanilla latte. unless there's a freaking pandemic. Depending on the space available for a bio, for example, I might remark about penning stories while watching deer in my back yard. It gives readers a glimpse into my writerly life.

Likewise, you'll want to set up an author profile on BookBub, Barnes & Noble, and Goodreads. Add the same photo and headshot for consistency and simply copy and paste your bio. Share these links online, and ask readers and fellow authors to follow you. And ask more than once! Don't count on all of your contacts being online the day you make the request. Once you're published, you'll discover some readers only post reviews to Goodreads while others prefer Amazon, Barnes & Noble, or BookBub. If you're lucky, the reader will copy and paste their review to every site.

SAMPLE BIO(s)

In addition to social media, you'll want a professional bio on your website and toward the back of your book. Remember to keep it updated as you write new books or win awards. I admit it takes a while when you add your bio to every social media page, website, and blog but it's worth the effort. If a newspaper or television station hears about your work and peruses your website, you definitely want them to read about your most current work and achievements.

I use three bios—one longer, detailed bio for my website, a shortened version for query letters, social media pages, or press releases, and yet another really short version for the back of books or for magazine articles I've written. The reason for having at least three different-sized bios is simply space allotments. Below are examples of mine.

You'll notice the important information is in the first couple of paragraphs. The last paragraph shows more of my personality or hobbies, and contact information. As previously mentioned, readers enjoy getting to know the writer behind the keyboard.

Bios should be written in third person, i.e., Beth Carter this and Beth Carter that. You'll also want to drop your first name after you introduce your full name and interchange "Carter" with "the author," so it's not tedious. Always add your website at the end.

Beth Carter, Author

Formerly a bank vice president and a hospital public relations director, Beth Carter had a mid-life crisis at a certain age and shed her suits and heels to reinvent herself as a writer. She now pens humorous women's fiction, romantic comedy, children's picture books, and a gold-medal-winning cookbook.

The author doesn't miss the 8 a.m. meetings whatsoever and prefers writing at Starbucks, or at the kitchen table. Carter has written the popular *Coconuts* series: *Thursdays At Coconuts, Chaos At Coconuts* (Book 2), *Babies At Coconuts* (Book 3), *Cowboys At Coconuts* (Book 4), *Brides At Coconuts* (Book 5), *Sleeping With Elvis, Miracle On Aisle Two, Santa Baby*, a novelette, and *The Quarantine Cookbook*, as well as *I Wrote A Book. Now What?* and coming soon: *I'm Published. Now what?*

Winner of a 2020 gold medal for THE QUARANTINE COOKBOOK, a 2020 silver medal for *Miracle On Aisle Two*, multiple Raven Awards in 2017-2019, and a RONE Award for *Thursdays At Coconuts* in 2015, when Carter was voted Best Debut Author by BTS Books.

The author's children's picture books include *What Do You Want To Be?, Sour Power, The Missing Key, and Santa's. Secret.* Her work also appears in four six-word memoir collections and numerous anthologies.

Splitting her time between Missouri and Florida, Beth Carter enjoys connecting with readers and has a private reader group, Beth's Book Babes, on Facebook. When she isn't writing, she's often found at T.J. Maxx, boating, or watching deer in her backyard. www.bethcarter.com

See, that's a really long bio but is fine for my website. It gives readers my background, a list of my current books, awards, a splash of my personality and where I'm from.

A shorter version

Beth Carter is a multi-award-winning novelist and children's picture book author. She has penned the popular Coconuts series, standalone novels, novellas, a cookbook for charity, and two books on writing. Carter divides her time between Missouri and Florida. www.bethcarter.com

An even shorter version:
Beth Carter is a multi-award-winning novelist, children's picture book writer, and cookbook author. Formerly a bank VP, Carter divides her time between Missouri and Florida. www.bethcarter.com

GET PROFESSIONAL HEADSHOTS

As already mentioned, professional headshots are necessary for a variety of reasons, including:

- ✓ Your Website
- ✓ Social Media Platforms
- ✓ Your Book's Back Cover
- ✓ The Interior of Your Book (*A Note From the Author*)
- ✓ For Magazine or Newspaper Articles

Often, there's a photographer at writer conferences. That's where mine were taken. My favorites are where I'm wearing bright clothing (red or royal blue.) Naturally, I wore classic black in my most current headshot. If you cannot get to a conference or cannot afford professional photos, have someone take a head and shoulders shot of you with a clear background. Have fun and try to relax during the photo shoot. I have one picture with my hands on my hips, one laughing, another with my hands under my chin, and a couple looking over my shoulder. Try different angles and let your personality shine.

FORM A FOCUS GROUP

While writing my first novel, I was torn between three possible titles and also craved early reader feedback. I was probably at the 50,000-word mark and wanted to know if I should continue writing. Of course, I didn't have any actual readers at the time because it was my first effort, and I didn't have a publisher.

While toiling away in my office, one day I had an aha moment.

I decided to invite seven girlfriends to our house so I could form my own focus group. After working in marketing for nearly two decades, I knew advertising agencies often had focus groups to test ads and marketing campaigns. Companies paid thousands of dollars for these invaluable opinions. Pollsters also do this often. I decided to create my own focus group, emailed my friends, and told them the task at hand. I promised to ply them with wine and offered simple appetizers. They all agreed to come and were excited about the prospect of reading my work and being my first set of eyes.

As I prepared for my friends' visit, I printed my first three chapters and made copies for everyone. I also created an anonymous survey for them to vote on three possible titles. *Thursdays At Coconuts* won, which was my favorite. I also asked my friends to rate my characters, the plot, setting, dialogue, you name it. While they intently read my chapters and filled out the typewritten survey, I paced our kitchen, heart pounding, and wineglass in hand.

All authors crave—but are terrified—of any critique from early readers. With the first book, it's exponentially more frightening. Like horror novel scary. After everyone returned their surveys, which I promised to read after they left, they happily chatted about my book. They all sounded excited. *Excited!* I was over the moon. My friends eagerly discussed my premise, characters, and said they wanted to read more. They wanted to know what was going to happen, especially with the bride and the banker who gets involved in a dubious way with a cop. That's all I needed to hear. I almost wanted them to leave so I could begin writing immediately. But I was a good host and waited until the following morning.

I encourage you to form your own focus group with friends and colleagues for this type of invaluable feedback. You could do it online, but it's much more fun in person. And...go ahead and ask your mom but you already know she'll say it's the best thing she has ever read.

CHOOSE A UNIQUE TITLE

Some writers think coming up with a title is torture. I happen to enjoy the process and have a difficult time writing a book until I decide on a name. I'm not saying I don't agonize over which one I'll eventually use, but I enjoy the creative process. Once I come up with five to ten titles, I ask for input from trusted readers in my reader group by posting the names in a poll and asking them to vote. As the author, I make the final decision, of course, but usually, the readers' favorite, is mine as well.

Visualize your title, fonts you like, and consider what elements you want on your cover. Depending on the genre you're writing, the title and mood of the cover will help you stand out from the millions of books on Amazon. The goal is to get noticed, which results in sales.

Here's an important tip: The minute you think of a title, Google it. You do not want another *Second Chances* novel. Nothing against that title. I, in fact, wanted to use said title ten years ago, but my publisher wouldn't let me. Why? Because my novel would have gotten buried in the search. Books with the same title by bigger-name authors would have popped up first in a Google search or while scrolling through thumbnail covers of books on Amazon or Barnes & Noble. As hard as you've worked on your manuscript, you don't want readers to confuse your work with another, bigger-name author who has already used the same title. When they click "Buy," make sure it's your book.

If you're writing a series, you may wish to ensure your readers know all of your books are connected by consistently using one word in each book title. I've seen this done many times. The common word could be a day of the week, a number that builds as the series grows, or a singular word that showcases your book, i.e., "Brides."

For example, in my *Coconuts* series (that's a bar/Happy Hour hangout, by the way,) I used Coconuts in every title to brand the series. If you intend to write a series, this is an easy way for readers to know the books are linked. This applies to nonfiction books as well, if they're not a standalone. My nonfiction books include my pandemic project for charity, *The Quarantine Cookbook*, this book, and its follow-up *I'm Published. Now What?* More about that much later. You'll notice I used two words, *Now What?*, in both titles. Again, the purpose is to connect them for the ease of readers.

With children's books, it's important to think of a title that will resonate with parents, teachers, kids, and the illustrator. You already read a list of my kidlit titles in my bio, so I won't repeat them here. I have many more in the pipeline. There just aren't enough hours in the day.

Good luck coming up with the perfect title for your novel, memoir, how-to book, poetry, short story collection, or whatever you're writing. Have fun with this challenge, research other titles in your genre, and request feedback.

CREATING TAGLINES

What are taglines? They're short, compelling descriptors of your novel or nonfiction book. They can also be considered a hook or an elevator pitch (should you happen to get stuck in an elevator with a big-time agent. It happens.) I know one woman who followed an agent into the restroom to pitch her novels. I wouldn't do this unless you happen to share the same sink, hit it off in other ways, and happen to mention that you'd love to pitch to said agent when it's appropriate. Let him or her ask for the pitch.

Back to taglines. They're important to have in an author's cache, but for some reason, they seem to incite nearly as much fear in authors as the back-cover blurb or a synopsis. Honestly, they aren't that difficult—just shorter.

Since I worked in marketing for many years, I think they're an exciting challenge. In banking and healthcare, I created branding campaigns, billboards, 30-second radio and television spots, and slogans, which is basically the corporate name for taglines. You may also hear them called loglines. When the hospital where I worked changed names, we decided we needed a new slogan. I made several attempts but decided to get everyone involved by holding a contest. I announced the winning department would receive a pizza party. I knew that would do the trick, plus pizza is much cheaper than hiring an advertising company. I put the word out via our employee newsletter and emails, and received about a hundred potential slogans. Many were good. I whittled them down to my five favorites and asked everyone to vote. During voting, I kept the names of everyone who participated anonymous. The winning slogan was: "We put the *care* in healthcare." The chief of surgery submitted it.

Isn't that cool?

Taglines should be short and catchy. Only use a sentence or two. Think of them as a mini advertisement for your book. Begin by writing down words that describe your novel, including the setting, plot, and characters. If it's nonfiction, consider your product, service, or widget. You'll want to evoke the theme and tone of your work. Is it a self-help guide, a paranormal, a political thriller, or a sweet (or steamy) romance? Consider all the elements and make a list. Study the various words which describe your work. This will help you create a memorable tagline.

Here are taglines I've created over the years to market my novels. I write women's fiction and contemporary romance with plenty of humor, heart, and a splash of suspense.

Thursdays At Coconuts
BFFs, sexy bad-boy cops, hippies, and neurotic brides. What could go wrong?

Chaos At Coconuts
Suzy, Alex, and Hope are baaack.
But who's the flashy newcomer? Wait. There's a tornado too?

Babies At Coconuts
For fans of *My Big Fat Greek Wedding* (Italian-style!) meets *Modern Family*.

Cowboys At Coconuts
Two worlds collide when a socialite plants a kiss on an unsuspecting cowboy.

Brides At Coconuts
A rushed proposal. A jilted bride. A shocking DNA test.

Just another day at Coconuts.

Miracle On Aisle Two
Sometimes the worst Christmas becomes the best.

Sleeping With Elvis
A deadly storm, rogue boyfriend, Elvis impersonator, and a cursing parrot. Now what?

Santa Baby
"Joy to the—"
Push. *Push.* The baby's coming.

As you can see, sometimes I use one-sentence taglines, and sometimes, two sentences. I've also used comparable movies or television shows, as well as dialogue to pitch my novels. Mix it up and play around with various words and sentence order. It'll come to you. I promise.

Another option is to get your family, friends, and readers involved in the conversation, like I did with my initial focus group. I often involve readers, give them at least five of my favorite options, and ask them to vote. One or two taglines always rise to the top. This accomplishes two things. Readers serve as your personal advertising agency, plus it generates excitement and goodwill among your fans.

FIND YOUR WRITING RHYTHM

Balancing marketing and writing is often a formidable feat. I hear many authors discuss this struggle. I'm one of them. You know how athletes, musicians, and dancers find the best time of day to train? Writers should do this as well. We also need to learn how to juggle the task of marketing with the joy of writing. Wait. That doesn't sound quite right. Marketing is fun too. Embrace it because we don't have any choice in the matter if we want to sell books to anyone besides family and friends.

Here's a fun example of finding your rhythm. I'm dating myself with this. My mom was a huge Elvis fan, and I definitely inherited that gene. In fact, I saw him in concert two months before he passed away. He appeared pale and bloated, but his voice was as strong and velvety as ever. Reportedly, Elvis preferred to jam all night with his band and sleep during the day. This would not be my preference, although I have been known to jot down notes before falling asleep or in the middle of the night.

I am not in the #5amwritingclub and likely never will be unless my hormones do an about face as I age. I've tried to talk myself into this schedule, saying I'd have the rest of the day to be free. But, no, not this girl. As I've already mentioned, I'm a stubborn #afternoonwriter through and through. I've found my most creative time is between two and six in the afternoon. I am a pretty fast writer and can fairly easily write two thousand words in a few hours.

To find your writing rhythm, you should try writing in the morning, afternoon, and evening. It may be hit and miss for a while, but you'll eventually find when you're most productive. And for those of you who have full-time jobs, young families to get off to school and assist with homework, you may have to settle for squeezing in writing when you can—early mornings, during lunch, or after everyone has gone to bed. I know several writers who do this and they've managed to write several books. It's doable. Find your most productive time and be consistent.

After you find your sweet spot for writing, make time for marketing during other parts of the day. If your best time to write is in the morning, then try marketing a few afternoons a week. And vice versa if you're an afternoon writer.

MANAGING SOCIAL MEDIA PLATFORMS

There are many social media sites vying for everyone's attention. They're fun and engaging, plus it's a great way to meet potential readers or talk shop with fellow authors.

The downside is spending too much time online, which I refer to as my water cooler, since writing is an extremely solitary profession, something that isn't taught in college lit classes. I truly think that's why many storytellers bow out. It's difficult to chain yourself to a chair day in and day out. Some days I ponder the fact that I create other worlds—escapism—for people to enjoy, yet here I sit at the table. *Again.* It must be because I love this career. And unless you live with a writer, musician, or another artist, they may not understand this weird obsession you have with your laptop, but I digress.

Back to managing your time online. I've heard many authors discuss the conundrum of balancing social media versus losing writing time. I'm guilty of this, but I'm getting better. Instead of a resolution last year, I chose the word "Balance." See, husband and family. I'm trying.

Some authors use extreme measures to protect their writing time. I know a few who use software with a kill switch that, like it or not, shuts down their social media, forcing them to only use Word, Scrivener, or whatever writing software they prefer. Kill switches are also used for safety measures. It's not a bad idea, but I keep telling myself I surely have enough willpower to sign off. Some days I do; some days I don't.

Social media sites come and go, and there will likely be

new ones by the time this book is published. Right now, here are the most popular social media apps and platforms that I hope you're already familiar with. It's a great way for a complete stranger to get to know you online and to take a chance on your book once it's published.

Facebook – We all know what this social networking giant is about. You've probably been on it for years. If you have a personal page, make sure to create an author page too. Be sure to mix up your posts. Share photos of your kids, grands, and pets as much as you talk about your books. Readers want to get to know *you*. Recipes are popular too. Talk about your writing process, hobbies, hometown, school, or anything that will enable future readers to relate to you. Build relationships. If you discover you both attended the same high school or college, your classmates just might buy your book or at the very least share your new release announcement with their followers. And reciprocate. Share their news as well. Wish your online friends happy birthday and happy anniversary. Comment on their posts. Interpersonal relationships, online or not, are a two-way street.

Twitter – I assume you're on Twitter, but if not, I'd join. Twitter has a supportive writing community, as previously mentioned. This platform is where hashtags come in handy. Short tweets are quick and easy. Be sure to provide tiny links for your books once they're published. Also, just like Facebook, mix up your tweets and don't constantly say "Buy my book." Be polite, thank those who retweet you, and return the favor. Some call others tweeples on Twitter, which is funny. I was recently called a tweetheart, which I thought was adorable.

Instagram – A photo-driven app, this site is a great place to showcase your book covers and personal interests. Hashtags are also popular on Instagram (IG). Once you set up a profile, study other authors' hashtags about books and the variety of ways they showcase their work or discuss writing. Be yourself and be creative. Some authors prop their book up beside their dog or cat to draw attention and be unique. I have an international reader who has posed with my books in Turkey, England, Scotland, and other countries. That's the kind of advertising you can't buy. Many of IG's users take advantage of using "insta" or "IG" with their hashtags, such as, #instaauthor or #authorsofig.

BookBub – I don't know if this is considered social media exactly, but it's an amazing, helpful site for readers and authors, plus it isn't time consuming. BookBub is a great place to establish an author page, showcase your books, leave reviews for other authors' books, and encourage readers to leave reviews for yours. They also offer marketing tips via newsletter. Finally, I've heard if you review other authors' books on this site, it will increase your own profile.

Pinterest – I admit I set up a Pinterest page five or six years ago and haven't looked at it since. I simply don't have time. I know many authors post their covers, inspiration for their settings, and even photos of male and female cover models. Some include actors who've inspired their characters. It's also great for recipes, so I really should update my page for my newer novels and mention my cookbook. Sigh. Can we get a 25-hour day?

Goodreads – I wouldn't say I'm a magician on Goodreads either. Far from it. I find this site hard to navigate. Maybe it's me. However, they have librarians who are happy to help. Goodreads offers giveaways for readers and you're able to post Q&A prompts on your page to entice readers— or possibly a book club—to inquire about your book. This is a great way to engage readers. Remember, Goodreads is a reader-focused platform.

LinkedIn – This site is much more business-y. If you're looking for freelance work or other writing gigs, I'd definitely suggest a profile page on LinkedIn. This is another site I haven't checked in a few years. It's simply impossible to interact on all of these sites and still find time to write.

There are many other platforms such as Tumblr, Snapchat, TikTok, and more. I'm not on any of them since I have to pick and choose my favorites. These sites appear to have younger audiences, so if you write Middle Grade (MG) or Young Adult (YA), they might be worth investigating.

This isn't an all-inclusive list, plus sites will come and go. Decide where you want to hang out and get started. I only frequent two or three platforms a day, plus my email. Otherwise, I'd never get any writing done. I'm most often on Facebook, Twitter, and Instagram.

I know I'm repeating myself, but watch the amount of time you spend online. I always seem to get sucked into the vortex and then get mad at myself if I've wiled away hours. Ideally, I prefer to spend an hour checking social media in the morning while I drink coffee and watch the news. I sporadically check it again later that day. That's my goal anyway. This is a do as I say, and not as I do chapter.

BUSINESS CARDS

This may seem obtuse, but writers need business cards. You're an *authorpreneur*. Don't you love that term? Embrace it. Writing is a business as much as it is pleasure, or anguish if you're the typical tormented writer-type. Just kidding. We all love it or we wouldn't do this, right?

You'll want business cards to hand to readers at book signings, conferences, work, for fellow authors, booksellers, and to give to complete strangers once they hear you're writing a book. Heck, my sweet husband takes a handful and gives them to his friends. Here's what you should include:

- ✓ Name
- ✓ Genre(s)
- ✓ Cover of your book
- ✓ Website address
- ✓ Phone number (optional)

I realize when you're starting out you may not have a book cover. In that case, make your name big and bold in a fancy font and get a small supply because you'll have a book deal soon. I believe in you. Be sure to use the same color scheme and any graphic details that appear on your website to ensure consistent branding.

BOOKMARKS

In my opinion, bookmarks are as essential as business cards. I realize many readers now read on Kindle or Nook but more than half still prefer paperbacks or hard cover books. Bookmarks make the perfect, inexpensive swag. If readers have your bookmark, it may remind them to check your website to see if and when you have a new book out.

I always include similar information and colors to coordinate with my business cards. I have several different bookmarks. Some are designed horizontally and others are vertical. I use different bookmarks for my novels than my children's books. They all include the cover of my books, taglines describing my book or at the very least the genre(s). Use the same pertinent information you include on your business card.

FINDING READERS

Writers won't get very far without a reader base. If you write great books, the readers will follow, I promise. But I hear you. You need readers *now* and are probably wondering how to connect with these wonderful people.

You'll find most readers lurking online just like authors. Pick and choose your favorite platforms, post inviting content, and use hashtags. I've discussed all three of those aspects (platforms, content, and hashtags) in other sections of this book.

Many times your readership will grow organically. Mine did. I began with about fifty or maybe a hundred readers—people I already knew—and now have several thousand fans, which is the weirdest, craziest, most wonderful thing, across all platforms. You can also find online book clubs and groups for a particular genre on Facebook or Twitter. For example, I'm sure there's a paranormal group, as well as a romantic suspense group. There's got to be a mystery and thriller page and a contemporary or historical romance page. I'm in contemporary romance, women's fiction, and chick lit groups. There are probably groups for engineering, medical books, law books, and cookbooks. You get the gist. Use that little search bar on Facebook to connect with readers who read the books you enjoy writing.

Also, please reach out and let people know you're there. It's annoying and a tad creepy when people only lurk online and never offer feedback. It's not that hard to mingle in cyberspace. Mention where you're from, who your favorite author is, what you're reading at the moment, and ask for book recommendations. Once you open up, you will be embraced in whichever community you're interested in.

PRICING YOUR BOOKS

If you land a traditional publishing deal, you can skip this section for now because your publisher will set the price. It'll likely be in your contract for both an eBook and a paperback price.

When you indie publish, you get the honor of setting your book's price. Be sure to research and see what price points other authors in your genre are using. You don't want to be too low or too high. Consider the options and realize readers will buy books from bigger-name authors like Nora Roberts, James Patterson, and Harlan Coben at much higher price points than they would a beginning writer. Those authors have paid their dues and readers know they'll be getting a good read. They take a bet on newer authors' books, so don't overprice your work when you're starting out.

Many years ago, some author or publisher had the fabulous idea of pricing eBooks at just ninety-nine cents. I'm being facetious about the fabulous part. Most authors gleefully jumped on the movement. Readers loved the cheap price and bought tons of books. Authors saw their stats on Amazon soar. But then, paying the bills using this price point isn't usually viable unless you sell thousands of books with each new release.

Sometimes I wish I knew who started this phenomenon of giving their/our work away. Doctors, engineers, and dentists don't cheapen their prices to less than a dollar. Nor do professors, artists, or sculptors. Even Starbucks refuses to sell a cup of coffee at that price. But now we've conditioned readers to expect free or almost-free books, and who can blame them? Heck, I love a bargain too.

I have noticed a trend over the past couple of years,

though. Some highly successful authors are beginning to raise the price of their eBooks by quite a lot. Some even price their eBook and paperback the same, even if it's $14.99 for each. I find that interesting. I've noticed eBooks selling for $5.99, $7.99, $9.99, and even higher. But, remember, authors who have a well-established platform also have readers who will buy everything they write. If you're new to this game, you definitely do not want to overprice your book.

There's another aspect to book pricing, and that's when you stay exclusively with Amazon and put your book in their Kindle Unlimited (KU) program. With KU, readers can read your book for free using Amazon's lending library. I can hear you gasping for air. Don't worry. You get paid about half a penny for every page read, and hundreds or thousands of reader clicks definitely add up. Getting paid by pages read is another reason to make sure your book is riveting out of the gate and keeps the reader enthralled. Think of it this way, this is a sales tactic to lure readers who wouldn't ordinarily read your genre or may be queasy about trying a new author's work. If they're unable to put your book down, they'll not only keep reading, which means more in your bank account, but they'll probably seek out your backlist, when you have one.

Qualifier: This does not refer to promotional sales for free or ninety-nine-cent books. Those are a great way to attract new readers or to bolster sales for an older book. This comes in especially handy if you pen a sequel, trilogy, or series and offer the first book for free or ninety-nine cents when the newest release is out. Some authors offer the first book in their series for free permanently. They call that permafree.

BOOK ELEMENTS

DEDICATION & ACKNOWLEDGMENT PAGES

Generally, most books have a dedication page and an acknowledgment page.

A dedication in the front of your book or novel is the time to thank those who have helped along your author journey. It may be a long-suffering spouse, a high school or college English instructor who inspired you, a child or a best friend who cheered you on along the way. It might even be a group of people like fellow critique readers, beta readers, or a writer's group that kept you motivated and sane. Usually, a dedication page is short and poignant.

Acknowledgment pages sometimes go in front after the dedication page but some authors prefer to place them in the back. I've done it both ways, and it may be at the discretion of your publisher.

To keep track of whom I want to mention on this page, I keep a file with the title of each book labeled "Acknowledgment Page." While I write the novel or book, I add to this page. Six months in, it's easy to forget someone who inspired you or provided an idea for your book. Having a ready-made file is an easy way to keep track, and it comes in handy when you're going through a flurry of second-round edits a few weeks before your release date. You'll be glad you kept this up to date and ready to go to your editor, even before she or he asks.

INTRODUCTION & TABLE OF CONTENTS

Nonfiction books often have an introduction and a Table of Contents. You would not see these elements in a novel, but they're valuable bits of information in the nonfiction genre. In an introduction, it's preferable to introduce the concept of the book, explain your journey, and why you're a good person to dispense the knowledge. Likewise, a Table of Contents makes it easy for readers to go to the section they're most interested in, though, we all hope every book will be read from beginning to end because we worked hard on it, plus you could miss something crucial. I draft a Table of Contents first, and then go through it carefully to make sure everything is in order because I'm famous for adding, deleting, and moving chapters around. See, I'm a pantser even when I write nonfiction. Some things never change!

PROLOGUE OR EPILOGUE

Prologues and epilogues are totally optional and occasionally controversial. My mother will not read a prologue for fear it will give the story away. I've never written one but have read many good prologues. I did, however, include an epilogue in one of my *Coconuts* novels. I wrote the epilogue for a pregnant character and chose to include an epilogue simply for timeline reasons. I wanted to have a baby reveal party and it needed to happen a few months after the book ended. At said party, my character announced the sex of the baby. One of my readers said it was one of the most well-crafted epilogues she had ever read. I guess I had beginner's luck.

Note: My editor mentioned while reading on a Kindle, books automatically open to the first chapter, which isn't ideal for authors who place important information toward the front. Consider this when you're deciding where to put certain elements. I am still old school and prefer paperbacks, so I wasn't aware of this issue.

SOCIAL MEDIA LINKS

Always list your website and social media links toward the end of each book. You want to make it easy for readers to find you and follow you on multiple platforms. This is a quick and easy process and a helpful way to grow your readership. I simply keep this page updated for any new social media links and copy and paste the links for each novel. You'll see mine toward the end of this book. Please follow me.

A NOTE FROM THE AUTHOR

I'm always a little disappointed when authors don't include a personal note at the end of their book, no matter the genre. It's up to you, but a simple three or four-paragraph note thanking readers for purchasing your book is a nice touch. Adding a headshot is even better. We're in a competitive industry, so I feel authors should make every effort to thank readers for their support.

INDEX

I added an index to my cookbook, but that's the only time I've used one. I've also seen indexes used in complicated nonfiction books and technical manuals. In that case, they're a helpful, needed guide.

Q&A SECTION

Occasionally, authors include a Question & Answer section to pose persuasive comments about their novel, characters, and their writing process in general. This is a great way to possibly attract book clubs. These sections are optional and are always toward the back of books. I've never included a Q&A section but I enjoy reading them.

BACK MATTER

After you've written more than one book, be sure to include an "Other Books By" page to cross promote your work. I've noticed these types of book listings both in the front and back of books.

Some authors use this area to provide an excerpt of the next book, especially if it's a series. Often, my publisher includes the blurb for each of my novels. The only concern is some readers think they have many more pages left in their novel before reaching the end and get upset if there's too much back matter, so don't go overboard with this type of information.

It goes without saying, every book needs a copyright page and a title page for when you have book signings and adoring fans.

SETTING GOALS

> "Believe you can and you're halfway there." ~Theodore
> Roosevelt

SET GOALS

Writers write differently, which makes perfect sense because we are diverse human beings. If everyone were given the same opening sentence, no two stories would be alike. If we were all given one word to use in a sentence, the sentences would be wildly divergent. Isn't that amazing?

I'll go out on a limb and say every writer loves words. Sometimes we love them so much that we have a hard time reeling ourselves—and our stories—in. Goal setting is important. Some writers prefer setting goals via word count or a set number of pages. For example, four pages a day equals 1,000 words since one double-spaced, typewritten page equals 250 words. Sorry for including math in a book about writing. Besides, your computer will indicate your word count.

Rather than number of pages, other authors, like me, set a block of time to write. I learned years ago that I'm most productive from 2-5 or 3-6 p.m. I'd like to start earlier but it never happens. I can easily write 2,000-3,000 words during that time. After that, my mind starts wandering, dinner is calling, and my wrists or back begin hurting. And those aren't perfect words, by any means. When my muse is on fire, I type as fast as I can. Editing comes later.

When I'm on deadline or have to turn around four hundred pages of edits in less than a week, I force myself to pull ten-hour days. I'm usually in wrist braces and taking Advil afterward, but I meet my deadlines. I couldn't keep up that rigorous timeframe week after week, though, I know several authors who do. As much as I enjoy writing fiction and escaping into another world, I equally enjoy real life and hope you take time to do the same to avoid burnout.

Goals are funny things. And they're personal. It doesn't matter how you achieve your objectives, just find what works best for you, set your own schedule, and stick by it. I've read this example many times: Writing one page a day, every day of the year, will end in a full-length novel. That's true. However, I, for one, don't want to work every day. When I worked in corporate America, I always had weekends off unless there was something urgent going on—I shudder when I remember our hospital merger—but working weekends was rare. If regular employees are able to take weekends off, I think writers should as well.

If you're one of those writers who writes many hours a day, seven days a week I'll cheer you on from the sidelines and even bring you coffee. Just remember to poke your head outside once in a while and join the living. I can almost guarantee every single time you force yourself to leave the house, you'll get an idea for a novel, see someone who would make the perfect character, or overhear juicy dialogue. Or if you're writing nonfiction, I bet you'll get ideas for inventions. I do nearly every single time I travel. I discover something that's lacking and want to create a widget. Maybe I'll get a patent like my husband. We're very competitive.

Back to goal setting. Reader demand may interfere with your goals, and that's a good thing. When I wrote my debut novel, *Thursdays At Coconuts*, I thought putting out one novel a year would be sufficient. I was wrong. If readers enjoy your work, they're immediately hungry for more, and they read quickly. Quite a few people read my novel over the first weekend and one woman stayed up until six in the morning to finish it. That was both thrilling and scary because I wanted to say, "Don't read so fast. I want to take a month or two off." But avid readers usually ask, er, demand a sequel, which is a huge compliment.

I was thrilled they wanted more, and as a pantser, I constantly overwrite, so I knew I could add a sequel in less than a year. Those two books were going to become a trilogy until I realized I had two meaty storylines and contacted my editor. She suggested I split the books and convinced me to divide them into two more books. I flipped the sequence of Book 3 and Book 4, which meant storylines were messed up and I had to do a great deal of rewriting and tweaking. It was a giant mess but it worked out and I've won multiple awards for this series. In the end, adding more books, dividing them, and reordering the series was the right decision, albeit as painful as ten hangnails at the time. I'm sure a lot of wine was consumed. Now, my *Coconuts* novels are a popular six-book series. But I'm moving on after Book 6. I really am, however bittersweet it will be. I hope reader demand forces you to go through the agony—I mean excitement—of adding a sequel or series.

Consider your goals. Right now, you may be focused on your very first book. I've never forgotten the exhilaration of my debut. I still get it with each book. I'm guessing you'll catch the literary bug and eventually write more than one book. Think about how many books you want to write in a year. Maybe you want to start out writing one like I did, then manage two books a year, and maybe squeeze in a third book on occasion. You may even be able to accomplish more per year. If so, great. Some of you will have fulltime jobs and young families. Others may be single parents or caring for aging relatives. Many of you likely squeeze in writing time during kids' naps, lunch hours, or late at night. Everyone's schedule varies. One of the best things about being a writer is getting to set our own schedule. You do you and have fun with it.

WHAT ARE YOUR OBJECTIVES?

Every author writes a novel or book for different reasons. Sometimes it's to tell the story of their heart. Other times it might be a professional who wants to share expertise on a certain subject. Some authors desire a career as a novelist, poet, cookbook author, or writer of short stories. Or a combination of all of these.

Consider your objectives. I'm a list maker, so I'm including several possibilities below to get your creative juices flowing. Think of your long-term hopes and dreams. Here are some options:

- ✓ See your novel/story/book/poem get traditionally published.
- ✓ Indie publish and have complete control.
- ✓ Write the story of your heart.
- ✓ Write a book and change the world.
- ✓ Enter contests.
- ✓ Win national and international awards.
- ✓ Have loyal fans.
- ✓ Receive a reader fan letter (or ten).
- ✓ Have a book signing.
- ✓ Connect with authors and readers at literary conferences.
- ✓ Be published in a literary magazine.
- ✓ Find an agent.
- ✓ Have amazing cover art.
- ✓ Become a bestseller.

✓ Have publishing houses bid on your manuscript at auction.

✓ Be on the *New York Times* or *USA Today* Bestseller List.

✓ Be a career novelist.

✓ Receive a patent on your product and write about it.

✓ Write academic books.

✓ Pen psychology-oriented books.

✓ Write for the fun of it.

✓ Have your book made into a movie or television series.

✓ Write drunk and edit sober, like Hemingway. Okay, this one was just for fun.

Which of these things do you want? *Really* want? Many are lofty, yet attainable goals. None of them are right or wrong. Some will probably come to pass while others may not, at least not for a few years or even a decade or two. That's okay. Whether this is your first, fifth, or twenty-fifth book, make sure you know your expectations and do your best to attain them.

OVERWHELMED? TRY THESE BASIC TASKS.

Every writer gets frustrated and wants to quit, hit the delete button, cry, scream, drink, or throw something. We've all been there. Occasionally, I get overwhelmed and think I cannot write One. More. Word. What helps? Don't laugh. Doing a simple task where I receive an immediate reward calms me. This may sound trivial but I'm betting at least one of these chores will help you too.

For a task to aid my process, I have to be able to visualize the mission. Writing a book can take nearly a year, and that's just the ticket to the dance. Afterward, there are several rounds of edits, cover art, rewrites, and marketing along the journey to become published. It never seems to end. Don't get me started on advanced marketing. That's for my next book.

Since you promised not to laugh, here are my calming secrets to abetting my creative frustration level:

Laundry – Beautifully folded laundry achieves my goal of emptying the hamper and making retail-like folds on the clothes. When I helped my parents out after my dad's knee replacement, my mother said, "I've never seen such beautiful laundry, but I don't have time for that." She also doesn't write, but she's a great proofreader. It's a running joke around our house. If I'm stressed about something like someone unexpectedly coming over, I'll start a load of laundry. Every time. My husband laughs and knows that's my reset button.

Mowing – Seeing the grass get shorter is an immediate reward, not to mention the benefits of vitamin D and getting outside. Bonus points if you are able to create pretty designs.

Emptying trash cans – It sounds lame, but when several trash cans are nearly filled to the brim, it stresses me out. After I empty them, the house immediately feels cleaner, and I can get back to writing.

Making the bed – Again, this is a simple chore but has a soothing effect afterward, plus your mother would be proud. And...you won't be tempted to take a nap and avoid writing.

Doing the dishes – A clean sink is much preferable to one piled high with dirty dishes. I know I have a touch of OCD like my character, Alex, but I can only take dirty dishes for so long—like fifteen minutes.

Organize something – I sorely need to organize my office—that's why I'm writing this book at the kitchen table—my closet, and a jewelry drawer. But I always think I don't have time when I know I'd be more serene if I'd just do it.

That's my list. What calms you when your nerves are frayed? Maybe it's watching a movie, reading, or baking. Do one thing a day that you can take charge of. Then, you'll be able to focus on your writing without household distractions. *Namaste.*

TRY WRITING SPRINTS

I absolutely love writing sprints. You can do them on your own or with fellow writers. I'm a competitive person, so I enjoy sprinting for thirty minutes—or for an hour—and comparing my word count with another author, but usually I'm so absorbed with my own work that I sprint alone.

Sprinting is an ideal way to increase your word count and achieve your goals. Before you sprint, refill your coffee or drink of choice. Go to the restroom, and set a timer. I use the microwave because I'm old school, plus I don't own a fancy smartwatch. Decide if you want to sprint for half an hour—my recommendation—or go longer.

Once you're finished, jot down your word count, stretch your fingers and legs, rinse and repeat.

While sprinting or on deadline, protect your writing time. Hide your phone, don't get on social media, wear tee shirts about writing, drink out of a writerly mug, or write yourself a motivational note—anything that keeps you in the zone.

If you sprint multiple times a day or week, I guarantee you will finish your book much faster than if you wait for inspiration. Don't wait for your muse to tell you when to write. Besides, she generally won't unless you're about to fall asleep or are in the shower. Then, your muse is wide awake. By setting a timer, sitting at the keyboard, and letting your fingers fly, the words will flow and your creative juices will awaken. I'm a fast writer, but never fear if you don't write quickly. It's always quality over quantity.

IMPOSTER SYNDROME

You will probably suffer from this literary affliction. Every author I know has imposter syndrome at some point in their career, if not with every single book. Even big-name authors who have written fifty books say they've agonized over this frustrating syndrome. Don't let it get in the way of your writing goals. Push through and kick imposter syndrome to the curb.

I had the phony condition while writing this book. Why? Because I know many authors who have written far more books, have a gazillion readers, make every bestselling list, teach courses on writing, and know more about marketing than I do. One thing I offer that these authors don't is *my* publishing journey and *my* background. My journey and stories are mine, just as your journey is yours. It's your story to tell.

I wanted to write a book that covered a multitude of topics for beginning writers including writing advice, inspiration, website information, building an online platform, grammar/punctuation tips, how to discover and query publishing professionals, and goal setting. I would have paid one hundred dollars for an all-encompassing craft book such as this in the early years of my writing escapades. I hope it has been helpful, and I'd love to hear which sections were most beneficial.

Don't give in to imposter syndrome, and don't fret if you get it. We all doubt ourselves at many points during our career. I think it's built into a writer's makeup. After all, we're putting our work out there for all to see and critique. Our work will be read by people all over the world, thanks to the Internet. I'm always astounded when I see reviews for my novels in other countries. For a while, my *Coconuts* series was quite popular in India, and I have readers in the United Kingdom, Canada, and of course, the United States. It's thrilling to know we all share the love of reading. Think about this: Authors create an eternal legacy. Let that sink in. Our words will live forever. That's a lot of pressure, but the rewards are worth it. Brush off the phony feelings of being an imposter, know you're in good company when those thoughts creep in, and start your next book.

A WINNING FORMULA

Years ago, I read this phrase in a writing magazine, probably, *Writer's Digest*:

BIC
HOK
TAM

It's perfect. I've seen this saying on coffee mugs and tee shirts. The phrase means:

Butt in chair.
Hands on keyboard.
Typing away madly.

Embrace it, and the words will follow. If we don't focus on our work, put away our phones, or lollygag around on social media, we'll never finish our projects. Trust me, our books do not write themselves.

AUTHOR CONFESSIONS

I have many author confessions which are subject to change daily. When I was an aspiring author, it would have helped my mindset—and blood pressure—had I known published authors felt the same way in their early years. I'm sure you'll be able to relate to some of my confessions, if not all. I also hope they provide much-needed inspiration and motivation. By the way, these are in no particular order.

- ✓ When I'm on a tight deadline, I may not wash my hair for a week. I'll often wear the same clothes three days in a row. That's a bit gross and may be too much information, but you probably already know by now that writers can be an eccentric bunch.
- ✓ Sometimes I'd rather stay in my fictional world—or nonfiction in this case—than face the real world. I can at least control my world, and I sometimes get annoyed when I have to leave it. Other times, I need a break. What can I say? I'm betting you'll feel the same.
- ✓ Some days I don't feel like writing. To be perfectly honest, some weeks I don't feel like it. But I usually write anyway. Occasionally, I can tell my mind and body—sore fingers and wrists, anyone?—need a break. I usually take December off unless I've written a Christmas book because we have thirteen adorable grandkids! I *know*. That's a lot and I'm not that old. Really. Anyway, I'm generally too overwhelmed with the holidays to add writing to my list. I also take a couple of

weeks off in the summer like normal people who go on vacation. Repeat after me: Writers need downtime too.

✓ I wish I had started writing sooner. I reinvented myself at fifty and have churned out several novels, children's books, a cookbook, this book, and multiple short stories and poems. But imagine how much I could have written if I had started earlier. Then again, I wouldn't have had the rich life experiences to include in my writing, so it all worked out.

✓ I haven't gotten many, thank goodness, but bad reviews haunt me to the point of obsession. I hate that those pesky remarks gnaw at me and try to override my many lovely, glowing reviews. Brace yourself. You will get a few bad reviews. Maybe even a terrible review, and it'll sting. A nasty comment may even keep you up at night. I've heard several authors say they never read their reviews. Some have assistants who only show them the glowing comments. I'm way too curious for that, plus reviews are a learning process—even the unflattering ones. See if you can glean something helpful from every review.

✓ I spend waaay too much money on author swag. What can I say? I love spoiling readers. It's also fun to see my book covers on unique items. But the boxes and boxes in my office. Oy.

✓ I sometimes wish I were a morning writer and had my afternoons free. After all of those years being a single mom, I just can't make myself rush around. My previous hectic schedule has obviously created a mental block for any early morning work routine, except for loading a dishwasher, starting laundry, scrolling social media, and checking email.

✓ Occasionally, I wish I had an assistant like many

authors, but to be honest, I think I'm too much of a control freak.

✓ I wish I weren't such a messy writer. I have scraps of paper, Post-its, napkins, and old receipts in piles everywhere. Each one will become a novel or a book. Sometimes, I'll take the time to put them in a file, but my brain is like lightning flashes. I have to get the idea down immediately or it's gone. It's a good thing I still remember shorthand from high school. I use it often. Yes, I'm that old. I keep tiny scraps of paper in baggies so they don't get lost. I maintain one nifty baggy per book, and if I'm lucky, I don't mix them up. And don't ask about all the times I forgot to look at said notes after penning "The End." Oh, well.

✓ On a similar note, I wish I were more organized. People who have spreadsheets and labeled files, whether hard copies or on the computer, amaze and astound me. Somehow I keep everything in my head. Maybe that means I'll fend off dementia. I hope so.

✓ I should spend more time marketing. I probably shouldn't say that in this book, but I'm being honest here. That's what a confession is, right? I actually enjoy marketing and know it's a necessity. But I love writing more. It's a balancing act for every writer.

✓ I need to cut my social media time in half. There. I said it. "Hello, My name is Beth and I spend too much time online."

✓ I had to stop writing this book because I couldn't decide whether to divide it into two books or simply shove a ton of information into one, large tome. That, plus a deadline for the last novel in my *Coconuts* series was looming. By the way, this will be two books. More about the second book later.

There. Thirteen author confessions. I could easily add a dozen more, but I don't want to bore you. I'd love to hear your confessions and am curious if some of yours are the same as mine. I bet they are. Always remember all authors have flaws and get frustrated. There are plenty of times when authors don't want to write, edit, query, market, or suffer from imposter syndrome. Just don't let these doubts grip you so hard that it paralyzes your writing. Write down your confessions on your laptop or on a piece of paper. Check back in six months and see what you've overcome, or if you still feel the same way. If nothing else, it's cathartic. I suppose I'll start cutting my social media time down tomorrow. Hold me to it.

NEXT UP: I'M PUBLISHED. NOW WHAT?

If the title above sounds familiar, it should. It's the sequel to the book you're reading now. See, I know you'll be published soon. I have faith in you.

While penning *I Wrote a Book. Now What?* I decided to divide my manuscript into two volumes. This book is for beginning writers who are early in their writing career, or even for those who may not have much of a platform because they skipped essential steps as they excitedly began their path to publication. I get it.

My second, more advanced book, *I'm Published. Now What?* will be for writers-now-authors who have pitched their books, have book deals, or have decided to indie publish. Still new to the publishing world, these beginning authors need assistance with more advanced marketing. Expect an action plan for your new release, plus a multitude of various marketing strategies, whether you promote your work exclusively online, in person at book signings and conferences, or like me, enjoy a little of both approaches.

When you're ready for my next book, watch my social media, website, or follow me on Amazon and BookBub for new release email alerts. I'm about half finished writing *I'm Published. Now What?* as of this printing, however, my publisher for the sixth *Coconuts* novel is waiting. And waiting. Yet another deadline looms. Welcome to the wonderful world of publishing.

OTHER BOOKS BY BETH CARTER

Novels
THURSDAYS AT COCONUTS (Book 1)
CHAOS AT COCONUTS (Book 2)
BABIES AT COCONUTS (Book 3)
COWBOYS AT COCONUTS (Book 4)
BRIDES AT COCONUTS (Book 5)
Book 6 releases soon. Don't miss this award-winning series!
SLEEPING WITH ELVIS
MIRACLE ON AISLE TWO
SANTA BABY (In the holiday anthology, SIZZLE IN THE
SNOW)

Nonfiction
THE QUARANTINE COOKBOOK
I WROTE A BOOK. NOW WHAT?
I PUBLISHED A BOOK. NOW WHAT? (Coming soon.)

Children's Picture Books
WHAT DO YOU WANT TO BE?
SOUR POWER
THE MISING KEY
SANTA'S SECRET

FOLLOW ME ON SOCIAL MEDIA

I love meeting readers and fellow authors. I hang out often at these online watering holes. Please follow me, and I'll return the favor.

Website: https://bethcarter.com

Facebook: https://www.facebook.com/authorbethcarter

Twitter: https://twitter.com/bethcarter007

BookBub: https://www.bookbub.com/authors/beth-carter

Instagram: https://www.instagram.com/bethcarterauthor/

Amazon Author Page:
http://amazon.com/author/bethcarter

Goodreads:https://www.goodreads.com/author/show/5796243.Beth_Carter

AN INVITATION TO JOIN BETH'S BOOK BABES

I'd love for you to join Beth's Book Babes, my private reader group. You can see how an online reader group is run while interacting with other like-minded authors and readers.

In my group, I discuss my humorous, heartfelt women's fiction, romantic comedy, nonfiction, children's books, and my pandemic cookbook. I provide a sneak peek behind my writerly curtain, discuss my process, request reader input, give Babes the exclusive on seeing my cover reveals, blurbs, and taglines. I also host contests, giveaways, and chat about reading and writing, of course. I've even held get-togethers for Beth's Book Babes in Missouri and Florida.

I think you'd enjoy my friendly, lively group. Members are social, supportive, and positive. Reading and writing are key, and bonus, it's a no-politics zone. Babes represent many different states and countries.

Request membership via the contact page on my website at www.bethcarter.com or simply type Beth's Book Babes in the Facebook search bar. It's that easy. I'd love to welcome you to our group.

A NOTE FROM THE AUTHOR

Thank you for reading *I Wrote a Book. Now What?* I hope several—if not all—sections were beneficial. As background, I had planned to write this book almost ten years ago. I'm glad I didn't because I learn something new about writing and publishing seemingly every day. I know far more now than I did even one year ago, and I predict you'll be the same.

Writing is a craft that free flows, uses our imagination, and enables us to create exciting new worlds, compelling memoirs, beautiful poetry, short stories, or helpful advice. Just like any instrument, it needs to be studied. Pianists take lessons; singers practice in studios—or in the shower; painters or sculptors perfect their art; engineers and architects fret over every design detail. Writers also need to hone their craft, which is exactly what you're doing by reading books about writing. Cheers to you!

Even though the writing industry is ever changing, remember you are in charge of your own destiny. You create sentences, scenes, and chapters that become books. Each page is another step on this exhilarating journey. Have fun and enjoy the ride.

I appreciate your support and hope you garnered helpful pearls of writing advice, inspiration, and motivation, as well as pitching, website, and marketing strategies. I would be thrilled to hear from you and learn which sections were most useful. An honest review on Amazon would be greatly appreciated. Hey, I had to ask. You should do the same with your books.

While writing is a solitary journey, it's a supportive environment. Be confident. Be professional. Be persistent. Congratulations, storyteller! You're on your way to becoming a published author. I can't wait to hear about your success.

Happy writing,

Beth Carter
Multi-Award-Winning Novelist & Children's Author
www.bethcarter.com

Made in the USA
Las Vegas, NV
01 June 2021

24011090R00109